CAMBRIDGE FIRST CERTIFICATE SKILLS
Series editor: Sue O'Connell

CAMBRIDGE FIRST CERTIFICATE
Grammar and Usage

Bob Obee

CAMBRIDGE
UNIVERSITY PRESS

Contents

Acknowledgements

I would like to thank the Series Editor, Sue O'Connell, for her invaluable comments and guidance, my editor Jeanne McCarten for her support and timely deadline reminders, Geraldine Mark, Brigit Viney and all the staff at Cambridge University Press involved in the production of the book. I should also like to especially thank Paul Carne, Jean Greenwood, Chris Hare, Ian Johnson, Laura Matthews, Keith Mitchell, Clare West and Simon Williams for their insightful comments and all teachers and students involved in piloting the material.

The author and publishers are grateful to the following individuals and institutions for permission to use copyright material in *Cambridge First Certificate Grammar and Usage*. While every effort has been made, it has not been possible to identify the sources of all material used and in such cases the publishers would welcome information from copyright holders.

Cartoons

Cartoons 1, 3, 5, and 6 on p. 47 from the *Spectator*; cartoon 4 on p. 47 by Hector Breeze © Hector Breeze; Garfield cartoon on p. 58 reproduced by permission of PAWS, INC.

Photographs

Photograph on p. 41 from the *Bank of England Museum: A Souvenir Guide* © Governor and Company of the Bank of England; photograph on p. 57 by permission of Rosamund Richardson; photographs of diving tank, snorkel and flippers on p. 73: Mark Gascoigne; photographs on p. 73 of Sarah Ferguson, Mikhail Gorbachev (photograph © Vitaly Armand/AFP), Princess Diana, Mao Tse-Tung, kangaroo, George Bush, Sydney Opera House (photograph by Cleland Rimmer): Popperfoto; photographs on p. 73 of Anthony Hopkins (in *The Remains of the Day*): Ronald Grand Archive/© 1993 Columbia Pictures Industries; Jack Nicholson (in *One Flew Over the Cuckoo's Nest*): Ronald Grant Archive; photograph on p. 73 of sun-dial: Sam Greenhill/Sally and Richard Greenhill; photograph on p. 73 of joy-stick, floppy disk and mouse: Sally and Richard Greenhill; photograph on p. 73 of egg-timer: Pictor; logos on p. 73 by courtesy of Esso UK plc, Jaguar Cars Limited, BP Oil International, La Chemise Lacoste; photograph on p. 89 of Brian Blessed: Gary Trotter/Rex Features; photographs on p. 109, skier: F. Witmer/Stockfile, 1: (photograph by J. Carter); 2: Interstock/Spectrum; 3: R. Symons/Spectrum; 4. Keith Mayhew; 5: Dan Smith/All-Sport; 6, 7, 8; Sporting Pictures.

Text extracts

Adapted advertisement on p. 7 reprinted with permission from Brooke Bond Foods Ltd; extract on p. 23 adapted from *The Hip and Thigh Diet* by Rosemary Conley published by Arrow Books Ltd; all entries on p.25 and entry for *make* on p. 133 from the *Collins COBUILD English Dictionary* © William Collins & Sons 1987, with the permission of HarperCollins Publishers Ltd; extract on p. 32 and extracts 3 and 4 on p. 68 adapted from *The Guinness Book of Records 1987* © Guinness Publishing Limited 1986; extracts 1, 2, 5 and 6 on p. 68 adapted from *The Guinness Book of Records* © Guinness Publishing Limited 1993; extract on p. 33 adapted from *The Long Day Wanes* by Anthony Burgess, published by William Heinemann Ltd, 1994; extracts on pp. 33 and 39–40 adapted from 'The Mekong' by Thomas O'Neill from *National Geographic*, February 1993; extract on p. 41 adapted from the *Bank of England Museum: A Souvenir Guide* © Governor and Company of the Bank of England; extract on p. 56 adapted from *Essential Thailand* by Christine Osborne, reproduced with the permission of AA Publishing; article on p. 58 from the *Daily Mail* © Daily Mail/Solo; extract on p. 59 from *Vegetarian Meals – A Sainsbury Cookbook* by Rosamund Richardson published by Martin Books; extract on p. 74 adapted from *The Day of the Triffids* by John Wyndham (Penguin Books, 1987) © Penguin Books Ltd, 1987; adapted advertisement on p. 82 © The Leisure Study Group Pty. Limited; extract on p. 88 adapted from 'Wide Open Wyoming' by Thomas J. Abercrombie from *National Geographic*, January 1993; article on p. 89 adapted from the *Evening Standard*, 23/2/99 © Evening Standard/Solo; extract on pp. 103–4 from *Athenscope – The Weekly Guide to What's On in Athens*, Issue No 25; translation errors on p. 110 © Addison-Wesley Publishing Co Inc; extract 5 on p. 112 and extract (e) on p. 119 from the *Guardian*; extract 2 on p. 112 and extract (a) on p. 119 from the *Independent*; extract (c) on p. 119 from the *Star* (Malaysia); entries for *tell* and *try* on p. 133 from the *Longman Dictionary of Contemporary English* (new edition) published by Longman Group UK Ltd 1987; article on p. 141 from the *Daily Mirror*; extract on p. 142 from ALTE, reproduced by permission of the Univbersity of Cambridge Local Examinations Syndicate.

Illustrations

Helen Humphries: pp. 3, 29, 30, 50, 82; Bill Piggins: pp. 11, 79, 123; Vicky Lowe: pp. 12, (top), 100; Amanda MacPhail: pp. 12 (bottom), 23, 31, 32, 47 (bottom), 48, 56, 66, 74, 81, 87, 96, 104, 111, 117, 118, 124, 140; Paul Collicut: pp. 21, 63, 116; Shaun Williams: p. 22; Angela Joliffe: p. 38; Jeremy Long: p. 47 (top right), 126; Tony Healey: p. 50; Tracy Rich: pp. 55, 98; Jerry Collins: p. 75; Tess Stone: p. 86; Sue Hillwood-Harris: p. 102; Paul Dickinson: p. 106; Mike Ogden: p. 131; Edward McLachlan: p. 139.

Facsimile artwork by Kevin McGeoghegan
Cover illustration by Annabel Wright

Map of the book

Introduction

Who is this book for?

This book provides grammar and usage practice for students preparing for Paper 3 of the Cambridge FCE exam. It can also, however, be used as a general grammar and usage workbook for students at this level. It aims to combine both general communicative grammar work with exam training; to serve students as a valuable grammar reference resource and, through its task-based approach, to improve students' grammar learning strategies.

How is the book organised?

The book is organised into eighteen units. Each unit focuses on a particular grammar area that is likely to be tested in Paper 3 of the FCE exam.

How is each unit organised?

Each unit is divided into four sections. The unit starts with a **Lead-in** section which introduces the language area to be looked at and sets students problem-solving tasks through which they can begin to explore some of the grammar and usage issues.

This is then followed by an interactive **Reference** section which, as well as highlighting the key grammar points and usage contrasts, requires students to fill in tables and grids, complete sets of examples and do a variety of exercises so that they become involved in the compiling of their own reference resource.

The third section is for **Communicative practice**. Students are encouraged to use the language which has been introduced in the two previous sections through a wide variety of lively and engaging task frameworks. The tasks involve contexts which encourage students to engage more personally with the language by talking about experiences and sharing opinions, deductions and what they know of the world with other students.

The unit ends with the **Exam focus** section. In each unit two types of exam question from Paper 3 or Paper 1 (Section A) are looked at. Paper 1, Section A questions are covered because its multiple-choice questions test grammar as well as vocabulary. The ways in which the language can be tested by each question type are presented and students are given useful exam tips on how to tackle each question. The Exam focus questions can be done in class or at home and all the Exam focus sections taken together provide thorough exam training for the grammar and usage parts of the Cambridge FCE exam. (The 'guided writing' question in Paper 3 is covered in *Writing*, another book in this series.)

How should the material be used?

The course can either be used in strict unit sequence or in a different order to coincide with a teacher's main course priorities and aims.

Each unit provides approximately two hours' class work. There is scope for flexibility in timings as certain tasks in the Reference sections and tasks in the Exam focus sections can be set for homework. The Teacher's Book also gives several useful ideas for follow-up tasks to main tasks.

What special features are there?

- The book begins with a **Foundation unit** which encourages students to think about their own grammar learning priorities as they approach the exam and raises some key issues about learning grammar and keeping grammar notes.

- Each unit begins with a **Summary** which highlights the grammar points and exam questions to be covered.

- The book includes numerous **Exam Tips** which indicate to students how best to tackle the different types of exam question.

- The book contains over forty stimulating **Communicative practice** activities to animate the grammar learning experience in the classroom.

- The book uses a great deal of authentic material so that students can learn grammar through genuine contexts.

- The **Teacher's Book** provides notes on typical student problems with each language area covered, practical suggestions on how best to exploit the material and guidelines on timing.

- The book finishes with a **Review unit** which provides a thorough revision session on each of the main question types in Paper 3.

Foundation unit

Language focus: what does learning grammar involve?; making grammar notes; ways of
learning grammar; using this book; types of exam questions

LEAD-IN

Each unit in this book begins with a Lead-in section which will encourage you to explore
what you already know about the grammar to be covered in the unit.

Read the questions below and choose the answers that match most closely your feelings
about learning grammar. Then plot your answers on the graph by drawing a circle around
the letters of your answers and joining them together with a line.

1 Grammar is

  A necessary but boring.
  B challenging and fun.

2 Making grammar mistakes

  A is the worst thing a learner can do.
  B can often help you to learn something.

3 Learning to use grammar correctly means

  A doing grammar exercises.
  B speaking and writing.

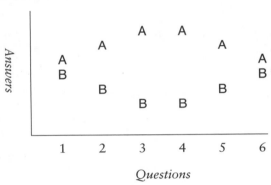

4 The notes you make on grammar

  A can never be as good as a reference book.
  B may make rules and examples more memorable.

5 The best way to learn grammar is

  A to learn rules by heart.
  B to see grammar working in real language situations.

6 Grammar is

  A cold and mathematical.
  B warm and human.

Now draw the shape of this line between
points 'x' and 'y' in the face.

What does this tell you about your feelings
about grammar? If your answers were all A,
or a mixture of A and B, imagine what your
picture would look like if they were all B.

Compare your picture with that of another
student. Discuss the similarities and
differences between them.

REFERENCE

The Reference sections in this book will give you concise explanations and lots of examples of specific grammar points. You will almost certainly, however, want to keep your own grammar notebook as you work towards the exam.

Below are extracts taken from two students' grammar notebooks. For each of the grammar points, decide which student you think has made the better notes and think about why. Discuss your answers with another student.

Student A   *Student B*

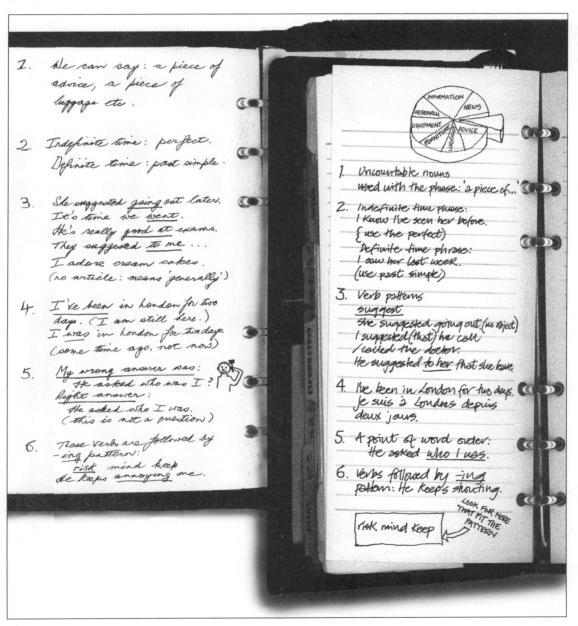

COMMUNICATIVE PRACTICE

The Communicative practice sections in this book will involve you in completing two or three tasks with other students. In doing these tasks you will have an opportunity to practise the language looked at in earlier sections in communicative situations.

1 Grammar activities and goals

As a student who is keen to learn grammar and as one who is approaching the First Certificate exam, choose from the list below the five most important things for you.

1 Revising grammar rules and looking at examples.
2 Seeing how grammar works in real texts and contexts.
3 Tips on how to learn grammar from reference books.
4 Learning how specific grammar points are tested in the First Certificate exam.
5 Communicating in speaking and writing, using the grammar you have learnt.
6 Getting specific tips on how to tackle grammar questions in Papers 1 and 3.
7 Doing grammar practice exercises.
8 Practising exam-type questions.
9 Checking how much grammar you already know.
10 Talking about yourself, other people and the world around us in English.

Now think about your choices. Do they tell you anything about your strengths and weaknesses as a learner of English? Discuss your choices with another student to see if you agree.

2 Using this book

As you work through the units in this book, you'll be doing all the things mentioned in Task 1. Look back at the ten types of activity in Task 1. With another student, try and work out which types of activity you'll be doing in each section (Lead-in, Reference, Communicative practice and Exam focus). You might like to look at Unit 3 as a sample unit. You may want to put the same activity into more than one section.

Lead-in: *1* ....

Reference: ....

Communicative practice: ....

Exam focus: ....

You should now have an idea of how the book works and how best to make it work for you.

EXAM FOCUS

This section of each unit focuses on how the language area presented in the unit is likely to be tested in the exam. In each section, two exam-type questions will be looked at and useful tips given on how to approach the question.

Question types

All the following types of question can occur in Papers 1 and 3 of the First Certificate exam. Look at each type of question and discuss with another student exactly what you have to do in each one. Working with another student, write instructions for each type of question.

1 Cloze

The number of people who wanted to join the navy was very high, but the number applying to join the air force was .... higher.

2 Transformation

a) I haven't heard from my sister in ages.
It's ages since ....

b) Scientists will carry out more tests in the near future.
More tests ....

3 Word formation

a) Why do you put up with his .... ?   RUDE
b) Our teacher was .... strict with pupils that were late.   BELIEF

4 Dialogue building

A: Excuse me. Can you .... ?
B: Yes, the train from Manchester is due in at 5.10.
A: Do you know if it's on time?

5 Telegramese

a) Sorry / I not write sooner / but / I not feel / well lately.
....

b) I be glad / hear / you recover / illness.
....

6 Multiple-choice

It's the first time that I .... here.
A am   B am being   C have been   D was

Unit 1 *The present*

Language focus: uses of the present simple and present continuous to talk about present time

Exam focus: dialogue building and telegramese questions

LEAD-IN

1 The text below is about the increasing number of people that are becoming vegetarians. Before you read it answer these questions.

– Are there any vegetarians in your country?
– Are more people in your country becoming vegetarians?

Discuss these questions with another student.

What are the two main kinds of reasons for people being or becoming vegetarians in your country? Choose from this list. Then compare your answers with another student.

economic   moral   religious   political
health   weight   none of these

2 Read the text and the questions about the numbered examples. Choose the right answers.

Healthy eating for vegetarians

Today more and more people (1) **are becoming** concerned about their diet, general fitness and lifestyle. Many (2) **are turning** away from meat and are starting to look for healthy alternatives. For some, becoming a vegetarian has provided an answer. Vegetables, fruit and pulses are healthy foods which can be made into hundreds of tasty meals; they also (3) **give** you plenty of energy and vitality to keep you going throughout the day.

If you (4) **are thinking** of taking the plunge, then you might be interested in a useful leaflet produced by Batchelors,

Healthy Eating for Vegetarians, which gives practical hints and tips on becoming a vegetarian. Fortunately, this (5) **doesn't mean** hours of slaving in the kitchen nor lots of menu planning. The two delicious snacks below (6) **take** less than ten minutes to prepare. Batchelors (7) **produce** lots of convenient and tasty foods, for those who (8) **don't eat** meat – just look out for the **V** symbol on packs, which means they've been approved by the Vegetarian Society. Batchelors (9) **are** also **offering** for this month only, 10 per cent off all vegetarian products.

(adapted from a Batchelors advertisement)

7

1 In Examples 1 and 2 the present continuous tense is used because the writer is talking about

    A a permanent situation.
    B a changing / developing situation.

2 In Examples 3, 5 and 6 the present simple tense is used because the writer is talking about

    A general truths.
    B something that happens every day.

3 In Example 4 the present continuous tense is used because the writer is talking about

    A a repeated or habitual action.
    B something happening around the time of writing.

4 In Example 7 the present simple tense is used because the writer is talking about

    A a permanent situation.
    B a developing situation.
    C a temporary situation.

5 In Example 8 the present simple tense is used because the writer is talking about

    A a temporary situation.
    B a repeated or habitual action.

6 In Example 9 the present continuous tense is used because the writer is talking about

    A a permanent situation.
    B a temporary situation.
    C a developing situation.

REFERENCE

Form

Present simple

Affirmative	*Negative*
I live, she lives, etc.	I do not (don't) live, she does not (doesn't) live, etc.

Question	*Short answers*
Do you live?	Yes, I do. No, I don't.

Present continuous

Affirmative	*Negative*
I am (I'm) living, etc.	I am not (I'm not) living, etc.

Question	*Short answers*
Are you living?	Yes, I am. No, I'm not.

Uses

Present simple	Present continuous
To talk about repeated or habitual actions. *Our meetings **don't usually start** until about 4.15.*	To talk about actions which are in progress at or around the time of speaking. *Look! The meeting is **starting**. We'd better go in.*
To talk about situations which are permanent or last for a long period of time. *'Where **do you work**?'* *'I **work** for Santax, a firm that **makes** mechanical toys.'*	To talk about situations which are temporary, but not necessarily happening at the time of speaking. *'What **are** you **working** on at the moment?'* *'A report for my boss.'*
To talk about general truths / facts / scientific laws. *Plants **do not grow** well if they are kept in the dark.*	To talk about situations which are in the process of developing or changing. *Michael **is growing** so quickly you won't recognise him the next time you see him.*

Verbs not typically used in the present continuous

The verbs below are not usually used in the continuous tense:

- like, want, wish
- agree, believe, care, know, mean, remember, suppose, understand
- look like, resemble, seem
- belong, contain, need, owe, own
- hear, see, smell, taste.

With the verbs **hear, see, smell** and **taste, can** is used to give the idea of *an action in progress.*

Can you taste the garlic in the soup? (Not: *Are you tasting . . . ?*)
*The windscreen is so dirty I **can hardly see** the road.*

1 Give a short definition of the words below, using a verb from the list above.

Example: *'Regret' is the feeling you have when you wish things had happened differently.*

1 'Property' is something ....

2 'Contents' are the things that ....

3 'Hard of hearing' describes someone ....

4 'A debt' is something ....

5 'Flavour' is what something ....

6 'Similarity' is a word used when someone / something ....

....

7 'A difference of opinion' is when two ....

8 'A synonym' is a word ....

Time words and phrases

1 The time word or phrase in a sentence is very often a clue to which tense to use. The words and phrases in the box below are nearly always used with the *present simple* tense to talk about present time.

always	as a rule	each / every time	ever	generally	how often . . . ?
most days	never	normally	once a (week)	rarely	regularly
sometimes	usually				

*The bus **usually** arrives at ten past the hour.*
*Our hotel does not, **as a rule**, cater for weddings.*

2 When talking about present time, the following words and phrases usually indicate that the *present continuous* tense, rather than the present simple, should be used.

at present	at the moment	currently	for now	for the time being
temporarily	this (morning)	today		

*Our phone isn't working **at the moment**.*

2 Underline the time expression in each of the sentences below and then complete them by putting the verb in brackets into the correct tense.

1 Each time I .... her to go out, she comes up with some clever excuse. (ask)

2 My sister .... some money as a lifeguard at the moment until she starts university.   (earn)

3 We didn't think Tony would be home. .... he .... today? (work / not)

4 .... he always .... his temper like that when he's losing a game?   (lose)

5 The bank .... normally .... open this late, but we're working different hours up to Christmas.   (stay / not)

6 We .... for now – we've decided we can't afford it. (move / not)

7 She .... better than ever this season.   (run)

8 .... you ever .... anything out of the ordinary? (do / not)

COMMUNICATIVE PRACTICE

1 They look the type

Look at the two columns of words between the pictures. Match a word on the left to one on the right to make a new noun and then match this phrase to one of the definitions below.

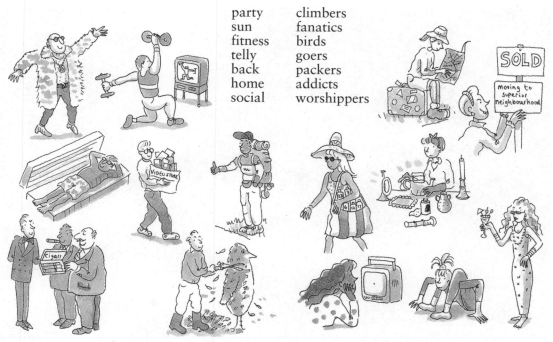

party	climbers
sun	fanatics
fitness	birds
telly	goers
back	packers
home	addicts
social	worshippers

1 .... are people who go out to parties and socialise a lot.

2 .... are people who want to improve their social position.

3 .... are people who spend a lot of time tanning themselves.

4 .... are people who spend a lot of their free time exercising.

5 .... are people who love to travel and see new places.

6 .... are people who do nothing but sit and watch television.

7 .... are people who spend most of their time at home.

Look at the pictures and, with another student, try and work out who is married to whom. Look for two people who clearly have something in common.

Example:

A: *I think the man who is wearing the fur coat and who looks as if he's having a really good time is probably married to the woman who's dancing.*

B: *What do they have in common?*

A: *They like going to parties.*

B: *Yeah, they're probably the 'party goers'.*

11

2 Customs around the world

Look at the map of the world and the pictures. Working with another student, find your way around the world as quickly as you can. Explain the custom connected with the picture in each country that you pass through.

Example: *In Canada Eskimos rub noses as a greeting and a sign of affection.*

EXAM FOCUS

EXAM TIP 1

Before and after

When you have a dialogue to complete, read through the whole text carefully before trying to fill in any of the missing lines. It is important to first work out the context of the dialogue. Then, when filling in your answers, pay careful attention to what is said in *in both the line before and after* the one you are trying to complete. Both can shape what you have to write.

1 Dialogue building

Amanda is looking for a flat to rent and is phoning an estate agent about an
advertisement in the local newspaper. The receptionist has put her through to Julia Kent.
In the conversation they have below, the parts numbered 1–8 have been left out.
Complete them in a suitable way.

Amanda:	Hello, I'm ringing about the advertisement for the flat in the Clifton area. Is it still available?
Julia:	Yes, you're the first person to ring.
Amanda:	Could I just check a few details with you then, please?
Julia:	Sure. What would you like to know?
Amanda:	Well, (1) ....
Julia:	Yes, its own bathroom and its own kitchen as well.
Amanda:	So it's completely self-contained?
Julia:	Yes, that's right.
Amanda:	And in the advertisement in front of me (2) ....
Julia:	Well actually, there is another room that you could use as a second bedroom but it's incredibly small.
Amanda:	I see. (3) .... there at the moment?
Julia:	No, no one. It's empty apart from the decorators who (4) ....
Amanda:	What kind of repairs?
Julia:	Oh nothing serious, repainting mainly. The last couple had a dog that caused a bit of damage. You (5) .... , do you?
Amanda:	Only a goldfish.
Julia:	The landlord shouldn't mind that.
Amanda:	When do you think I could see the flat?
Julia:	I'll ring the landlord now and call you straight back.
Amanda:	That might be difficult because (6) ....
Julia:	A phonebox. (7) .... ?
Amanda:	Yes, it does, but there's a queue outside.
Julia:	OK. I'll call the landlord and you can call me back.
Amanda:	Fine. Who (8) .... ?
Julia:	For Julia Kent or if I'm not here, Pam Reeves.

EXAM TIP 2

To somebody from someone

The telegramese question is always in the form of a letter *to somebody from someone*. As you read through the letter think about how well the writer knows the reader and the kind of information he / she is trying to give. Good friends, for example, know about each other's permanent situation and are more likely to write about things happening in their lives now.

2 Telegramese

Make all the changes and additions necessary to produce, from the following sets of words and phrases, sentences which together make a complete letter. Write each sentence in the space provided.

3 Hampton Grove,
Winchcombe,
Sussex

3rd March 1994

Dear Jenny,

1 We stay / my mother / this week / her house / in country.

....

2 Children love garden / play / out there now.

....

3 I adore / peace and quiet / never want / return city / when be here.

....

4 You see / sea / from bedroom / make you / feel so good / when get up / morning.

....

5 Adam take / week off / help my mother / paint bathroom.

....

6 We think / seriously / move here / if find / jobs.

....

7 There be / small factory / in town / employ / most people / live / here.

....

8 Anyway / we be back / London / weekend / call round / if you / have nothing / do.

....

Best wishes,

Sarah

Unit 2 Modals 1

Language focus: uses of modal verbs of ability and permission (in the present and past) and modal verbs of obligation and possibility (in the present)

Exam focus: cloze and transformation questions

LEAD-IN

1 Read the jokes and, with another student, find the punch line – in a–i below – that completes each joke.

1 During a lesson on the benefits of eating healthy food an enthusiastic teacher asked, 'Can anyone name five things that contain milk?'

2 A motorist and his wife had had a quarrel and hadn't spoken for hours. Suddenly the man saw a donkey in a field. 'Must be a relative of yours,' he said.

3 At a buffet dinner a husband said to his wife, 'You can't be going back for dessert again. That makes five times. Aren't you ashamed?'

4 At the sight of a submarine a baby sardine quickly hid behind its mother. 'You needn't be afraid,' she said.

5 On arriving home holding a brightly-coloured bag, a husband asked, 'What do you think I might have here for the one I love best?'

6 A struggling newspaper reporter asked his editor, 'Do you think I ought to put more fire into my stories?'

7 A maths teacher was explaining to students what they had to do to get the answer to this problem: 'You have ten fingers. Suppose you had three less. What would you have?'

8 A bookshop assistant, eager for a quick sale, approached a student and said, 'I guarantee that this book can do half your work for you.'

9 After hearing much yelling and screaming, a father burst into his sons' room to find them fighting on the floor. 'Okay, who started this?' he asked.

a) 'It's only a can of people.'

b) 'No, vice versa.'

c) 'You did. You told him he could hit me back,' replied the elder son.

d) 'Butter, cream, cheese and two cows.'

e) 'No music lessons.'

f) 'Not really. I just say that I'm getting it for you.'

g) 'Cigars, razor blades and a new electric drill.'

h) 'Yes, by marriage.'

i) 'Great, I'll take two of them.'

2 Each of the jokes in Task 1 contains a *modal verb*. Modal verbs are used in front of the main verb in a sentence. They can express ideas such as the possibility, necessity or certainty of an action happening. Look back at the jokes and underline the modal verb in each one. Then check your answers with another student.

Example: <u>*Can*</u> *anyone name five things that contain milk?*

3 Now discuss with another student which of the meanings below is expressed by the modal verb in each joke. Write the number of the joke next to one of the meanings.

1 ability (of a person/thing to do something) ....

2 necessity (Is it necessary or unnecessary?) ....

3 permission (Is the person allowed to do something?) ....

4 possibility (How sure is the speaker?) ....

REFERENCE

Form

Affirmative	*Negative*
I can, etc.	I cannot (can't), etc.
Question	*Short answers*
Can you?	Yes, I can. No, I can't.

1 Modal verbs do not change form. They do not take an auxiliary in the question and negative form.

2 Modal verbs are followed by the infinitive without **to**.
   You **must arrive** on time.
   You **needn't bother**.

3 We cannot use two modal verbs together: for example not *She should can go*. The second idea is expressed by a phrase such as **be able to** or **be allowed to**.
   She should **be able to** *go.*

Uses

Modal verbs express a number of different kinds of meaning. One verb can often express more than one kind of meaning. For example:

He can play really well. (ability)
Can I come in now? (permission)
You can't be serious. (possibility)

1 First see how many of the sentences you can complete by choosing the correct answer from the verbs in brackets. Then study Sections A and B and decide on your final answer.

1 Stephanie .... hear someone approaching and quickly hid behind the door.   (was able to / could)

2 'Could I borrow the car, Dad?' 'No, you ....'
(can't / couldn't)

3 The lifeguard arrived and .... save us.
(could / managed to)

4 .... your lawyer go with you yesterday?   (Couldn't / Could)

5 No one .... see the prisoner since Friday.
(could / has been allowed to)

6 The people that had been queuing outside the shop .... go in early.   (could / were allowed to)

7 I .... make any phone calls for over an hour.
(can't have / haven't been able to)

8 As we approached we .... smell something good cooking.
(could / were able to)

A *Ability:* can, could, be able to

1 **Can** and **cannot / can't** are more commonly used to talk about ability to do something in the present than **be (not) able to**.

*Mum **can't** drive at the moment because her leg is in plaster.*
*The doctor **can** see you right away, if you have the time.*

2 To talk about someone's ability to do something in the past we use **could, be able to** and **manage to** as follows:

General ability (to do something at any time)	could couldn't could you? *I **could** talk before I could walk.* *Could you really run that fast at school?*
Specific ability (to do something on one occasion)	couldn't was / were (not) able to (not) managed to *I **was able** to see the doctor without an appointment.* *Did you **manage to** phone the boss this morning?* (not: *could*) *I **couldn't** join the sailing club then – I was too young.*

NOTE: The verbs **see, hear, feel, smell, taste** and **understand** are an exception and are used with **could** to talk about specific ability.

*The guard **could smell** smoke but didn't know where it was from.*

3 To talk about ability with perfect and future forms, the **be able to** structure is used.

*The police **have not been able to** identify the body yet.*
*When **will he be able to** come home, doctor?*

B *Permission:* can, could, may, be allowed to

1 When asking for permission in the present we usually use **can** and **could**. **Could** is less direct than **can**. **May** can be used but is quite formal.

When giving permission we nearly always use **can**. Again **may** can be used but sounds rather formal.

*'**Could** I leave early as I've got an interview?' 'Of course you **can**.'*
*****Can** I call you back? I'm in a meeting at the moment.*
*****May** I use your phone, please?*

When talking about whether something is permitted or not we use **can / can't** and **be (not) allowed to**.

*Guests **can** leave their keys at reception or take them with them.*
*Don't you know you're **not allowed to** smoke during take-off?*

2 To talk about permission in the past:

General permission	could / couldn't was / were (not) allowed to *As a child I **could** always stay up late at weekends.* *We **weren't allowed to** wear what we liked to school when we were young.*
Permission in specific situations	was / were (not) allowed to couldn't *The candidate **was allowed to** ask a few questions* (not: *could*) *The security police told us we **couldn't** wait inside the airport because someone important was arriving.*

3 When talking about permission with future and perfect forms **be allowed to** must be used.

*You **will not be allowed to** bring notes into the exam.*
*He's **never been allowed to** travel alone.*

C *Obligation and necessity:* must, have to, should, ought to, needn't

2 Imagine someone is talking about going to a meeting. Match a sentence from the column on the left to one on the right which explains it.

e 1 You ought to go.   a) It would be a waste of time for you to go.
d 2 You must go.   b) That's the company rule.
b 3 You have to be there.   c) No one is forcing you to go.
c 4 You don't have to go.   d) That's an order.
a 5 You needn't go.   e) It would really help you.
f 6 You mustn't go.   f) It wouldn't be right.

Now check your answers by reading the information below.

1 Must is normally used when the sense of obligation comes from the speaker / writer.
*You **must** stop smoking for the sake of your health.*

Have to is used when the obligation comes from someone else or an external authority.
*We **have to** be out of the room by 12.00 – that's the hotel rule.*

Have to, however, has to be used when talking about obligation with future, past and perfect meanings.
*There were no seats left so some of the audience **had to** stand.*
*We **will have to** be going now in case it rains.*
*He's **had to** give up his job for health reasons.*

2 **Mustn't** is used to express strong disapproval, or that something is forbidden.
*You **mustn't** keep annoying your father. He is trying to work.*

Don't have to is used to express the idea that there is no law, rule or requirement to make you do something.
*I adore Saturday mornings when I **don't have to** get up for work.*

Needn't expresses the speaker's opinion that something isn't necessary.
*You **needn't** worry about the boat trip – it only lasts ten minutes.*

3 **Should** and **ought to** express milder obligation; they are often used when giving advice or talking about people's responsibilities.
*I really **ought to** be getting home – my daughter is expecting me.*
*You **should** always keep receipts when you buy large items.*

supposed to — a rule that may be disobeyed.

D *Possibility, probability and certainty*

3 Complete each of the rules below and their accompanying examples with a word from the box.

must	can	may	can't	might not	could	couldn't

1 (a) .... is used when the speaker is certain that something is true.

(b) .... is used when the speaker believes something is impossible or is certain that something isn't true.

That (c) .... be the Paris train – it's not due for hours.

I (d) .... be missing a page – this doesn't make sense.

2 **Should** and **ought to** can express the idea that something is probable or likely.

*You **should** be receiving a cheque from us in a few days.*

3 (a) .... is used to talk about the general possibility of something.

Leave early as the roads (b) .... be especially busy at that time.

May, **might** and **could** are used to express the idea of possibility in specific situations.

(c) .... can indicate stronger possibility than **might** or (d) .... and is not used to ask questions.

May not and **might not** are used to express the idea that it is possible that something is not true. **Could not** means that in your opinion something is not hypothetically possible.

*You **may** well be right about the cost but I'm still going.*

I (e) .... not be going to see her now that something's come up.

(f) .... he be using your credit card without your knowing?

4 Complete the following sentences with an appropriate modal verb form.

1 You .... possibly go out looking like that.

2 Your friend .... be able to get seats without too much trouble.

3 You .... bother phoning, just turn up about sixish.

4 .... you really buy a house that cheaply in those days?

5 I'm afraid I .... get petty cash requests approved by the manager.

6 He .... be joking! The car's not worth anywhere near that much.

7 It's not a good time to visit Britain. The weather .... be awful at this time of year.

8 Only the press .... visit the crash site yesterday.

9 Your parents .... stop you going to the concert, although I can understand why they're worried.

10 Martin .... need the car. Why don't you ask to borrow it?

COMMUNICATIVE PRACTICE

1 Treasure hunt

Look at the map opposite and find the place labelled 'Start here'. Then follow the instructions on the document below which was written by Pirate Scragg. They will tell you how to find his buried treasure.

~ The treasure of Pirate Scragg ~

Go to the point where the bird wouldn't stop if it flew straight to the pond.
And from here go to the place where you ought to cross the road.
Now take the quickest route round a place where you can sink but can't swim.
To a place where you can find smoke without fire.
From here go to a place where a pirate's feet might not touch the ground.
And then to a place where you can always expect to see white water.
Now pass an old pirate who needn't be feared.
To a place where you may hear singing and ringing.
Now you must retrace your steps with the line of a thick black pen.
Look at the shape you have drawn, and this shape should reveal the location of the
treasure in one of the places you didn't have to visit.

2 What's the law?

Look at the pictures below which illustrate eight different situations in Britain. Then look at the phrases in the box and, with another student, decide which phrase tells you something about the law in each situation. Then work out what the law might be.

Useful language when talking about the law:		
have to/don't have to	(not) be allowed to	can/cannot

legal limit	age of 16 or 18	age of 17	no law
licence	70	six months	age of 16

Example: *Picture 1 – licence.*

You have to buy a television licence each year if you own or rent a television.

Now you know the law in Britain, discuss with your partner whether it is different or the same in your country.

D EXAM FOCUS

EXAM TIP 3

Translating the gap

When there is a gap in a cloze exercise which you think is a modal verb, try translating the 'idea' of the gap into a longer phrase such as: **it is necessary / it is possible / certain / (you) are able to / (you) are allowed to.** This will help you to focus on a smaller number of reasonable choices.

Remember that words such as **can't / cannot / couldn't / won't,** etc. only count as one word and can therefore go in a gap where appropriate.

1 Cloze

The passage below is adapted from a book called *The Hip and Thigh Diet*. Here the author is explaining how to use the diet and talking about the results you can expect.

Read the passage and fill each of the numbered blanks with *one* word. Then check your answers with another student.

We think you (1) .... initially follow the menu selections provided here as a basic guide but as you become more familiar with the fat content of all foods you will soon be (2) .... to make up your own selections.

You have been given a list of strictly forbidden foods so that you (3) .... make a definite resolution before you begin the diet: 'I (4) .... ban them totally from my life!' If you are going to cheat and put bars of chocolate or packets of salted peanuts into your cupboard to eat when no one's around then you really (5) .... to give this book to someone else. This diet, if followed properly, will help you to achieve the kind of figure you never dreamed possible but there is only one person who (6) .... actually make it work for you – and that's YOU. You're the one that (7) .... to stick to it.

You will probably be very pleasantly surprised at the amount of food you are (8) .... by the diet. You'll find yourself on a strict diet without (9) .... to suffer in the process. My volunteers really loved it and they (10) .... believe they could actually lose weight yet eat so much.

(adapted from Rosemary Conley, *The Hip and Thigh Diet*)

2 Transformation

Look at the verbs in the box below and read the sentences. Match the phrase in bold print in each sentence with a verb in the box. Then rewrite the sentence using this verb, making all other changes necessary. The list includes some words you will not need to use.

should	needn't	might not	couldn't	be able to	can't
have to	must	be allowed to	could	don't have to	ought to

Example: **It's essential** that all competitors arrive on time.
must: All competitors must arrive on time.

1 **There's no need** for you to bring a present as well.

You ....

2 I'm surprised **permission was given** for Mrs Jones to have the day off.

I'm surprised ....

3 There's **no law that requires** drivers to wear seat belts in my country.

Drivers ....

4 I suppose **it's possible** her phone isn't working.

I suppose ....

5 **There's a chance** the hurricane will hit northern towns tomorrow.

The hurricane ....

6 **Did you manage to** get a copy of this morning's paper?

Were ....

7 It's always **advisable** to have medical insurance when you travel.

You ....

8 **It's not possible** for a person to lose so much weight so quickly.

A person ....

9 **It's likely** that Richard is on his way here now.

Richard ....

Unit 3 Adjectives and adverbs

> *Language focus:* uses of adjectives and adverbs; position and order of adjectives; forming
> adverbs from adjectives; position of adverbs
>
> *Exam focus:* word formation and cloze questions

LEAD-IN

1 Look at the two sentences below and say what parts of speech are underlined.

a) Sheila's a heavy smoker but still attends **regular** <u>fitness classes</u>.
b) Sheila's a heavy smoker but still <u>attends</u> fitness classes **regularly**.

Now complete these general rules for adjectives and adverbs.

i) Adjectives are typically used with .... and adverbs are used with ....

ii) To form the adverb from the adjective we usually add ....

2 There are, however, various exceptions to the above two rules. Look at the three kinds of exception in the box and then read through the dictionary entries to find at least *two* more examples for each box.

a) With some words, the adverb and adjective are the same, e.g. **hard** (*he works hard*). ....
b) With some adjectives, as well as adding **-ly** to form the adverb, there is also a change in spelling e.g. **probable – probably**. ....
c) Some verbs are followed by adjectives, not adverbs, e.g. **taste** (*it tastes funny*). ....

awful /ɔːfʊl/. **1** 1f you say that something **is awful**, you mean that it is 1.1 not very good or not very nice. EG *Isn't the weather awful?... Gas smells awful... The road is awful: narrow and bumpy... What an awful thing to say... ... married to that awful man.* **1.2** very unpleasant or very bad causing people to feel shock, fear, or sadness. EG *...an account of that awful war... My second husband had an awful death.* ADJ QUALIT ⇑ nasty = dreadful ≠ wonderful = horrific
2 If someone looks or feels **awful**, they look or feel ill. EG *I felt awful last night... God, he looks awful... My neck felt awful.* ADJ QUALIT = terrible = well

fast /fɑːst/ faster, fastest: fasts, fasting, fasted. **1** Something or someone that is **fast** moves, does ADJ QUALIT = quick, swift something, or happens with great speed. EG *...a fast car... ...fast communications... Relationships today tend to change at a faster pace than ever before.* = rapid = slow
► used as an adverb. EG *I ran as fast as I could... The music went faster and faster... News travels pretty fast... ...fast-flowing upland streams.* ► ADV + VB

happy /hæpɪ/, happier, happiest. **1** Someone who is **happy** has feelings of pleasure, for example because something nice has happened or because they feel satisfied with their life. EG *I was happy to hear that you passed your exam... This wlll make the children happy.* ► used of a person's expression. EG *...a* ADJ QUALIT ⇑ content = pleased ≠ sad ► = cheerful happy smile. ◊ **happily**. EG *We laughed and chatted happily together.* ◊ **happiness**. EG *Money did not bring happiness.* ◊ ADV ◊ N UNCOUNT

late /leɪt/, later, latest. **1 Late** is used to describe things that happen or are done near the end of a particular evening, day, year, etc. EG *She had stayed up late drinking vodka... ...in the late afternoon...* ADV. OR ADJ QUALIT ≠ early

tragic /trædʒɪk/ **1** Something that is **tragic** is very sad because it involves death, suffering, or disaster. EG *The most tragic sight of all was the very young addicts... ...the tragic death of hls elder brother Michael.* ◊ **tragically**. EG *He was tragically killed in a car crash.* ADJ QUALIT ⇑ distressing ◊ ADV WITH VB. OR ADV SEN

(from the *Collins COBUILD English Language Dictionary*)

REFERENCE

A Uses of adjectives

Adjectives are typically used:

1 before nouns
2 after certain verbs.

Adjectives before nouns

Where several adjectives are used in front of a noun there are clear rules about the order in which they should come.

1 Descriptive adjectives occur in the following order:
    size   age   shape   colour   origin   material
    *My cousin lives in a **large old Dutch** canal boat.*
    *The actor was wearing a **long red silk** scarf.*

2 Adjectives that express your opinion about something usually come before adjectives that describe the noun:
    *The necklace was made of **beautiful pink** glass.*

    If two 'opinion' adjectives are used, the more general one comes first.
    *We rented a **nice quiet** cottage by the sea.*

3 Adjectives used before nouns are only joined with **and** when the adjectives are of the same type, e.g. two colours.
    *The **black and white** rocket raced up into the clouds.*

1 **Read the sentences below and put the adjectives in front of the noun in the correct order.**

1 The museum houses several (Japanese / stone / ancient) vases.
2 The thieves used a (thin / long / wire) hook to open the door.
3 My granddad kept his money in a (tin / funny / old / red) can.
4 As he opened the cell door there was a (blinding / white) flash of light.
5 My mother always says that I was a healthy baby with (large / blue / round) eyes.

Adjectives after certain verbs — verbs g perception

1 After the following verbs we use adjectives, not adverbs:

appear	be	become	feel	look	seem	smell	sound	taste

*This apple **tastes funny**. Did you wash it?*
*I haven't had much sleep: that's why I **look so awful**.*
*The driver **became** really **angry** when I refused to move.*

Note, however, that some of these verbs can also be used with adverbs.

- **feel** with the meaning of 'touch' and in the phrase **feel well** to talk about health and illness.
  *The doctor **felt** her injured arm **carefully**.*
  *I really don't **feel well** – it must be the heat.*

- **look,** with the meaning of 'study / focus the eyes on'.
  *The referee **looked quickly** at his watch.* (study)

- **Appear** with the meaning of 'come into view'.
  *She **appeared suddenly** at the door.*

2 **Make, keep** and **find** are followed by adjectives when used in the following structure: 'verb + object + adjective'.
*I **find it difficult** to believe that she didn't phone.*
*The accident should **make him more careful** next time.*

B Uses of adverbs

1 With verbs:
*The police **moved quickly** to stop a fight between the fans.*

2 Before adjectives:
*The Divan Hotel has **reasonably priced** rooms.*

3 Before other adverbs:
*My penfriend replied to my first letter **incredibly quickly**.*

4 Before prepositional phrases:
*The plane shook and then went **completely out of control**.*

Forming adverbs

1 To form adverbs from adjectives we usually add -ly to the adjective: **slow – slowly, smooth – smoothly.**

2 **Good** is the only adjective with a completely irregular adverb: **well.**

3 For adjectives which already end in -ly, e.g. **friendly, cowardly, silly, ugly,** the adverb form is expressed by the phrase: **in a . . . way.**
*The stranger asked **in a friendly way** if he could stay.*

4 Two other kinds of exception to the rule are adjectives which have the same adverb form and those where there is a spelling change to form the adverb (see table on next page).

2 Put the adjectives below into the correct box in the table. Then add the adverb form of each adjective. Two have already been done for you.

easy   straight   simple   good   ordinary   terrible
far   comic   hard   specific   fast   lucky

Change of spelling	*Irregular form*	*Adverb form same as adjective*
easy – easily		straight – straight

3 Now by looking at the *Change of spelling* box write two more rules like the one below.

1 With adjectives ending in 'y', the 'y' is replaced by 'i'.

2 ....

3 ....

Position of adverbs

1 Adverbs normally go after the verb.
He smokes heavily.

2 An adverb does not normally come between a verb and its direct object.
He studied the book carefully. (not: *He studied carefully the book.*)

3 If two or more adverbs are used, they usually come in the order:
manner   place   time
*The plane landed **smoothly right on time.***
*Didn't the team **play well away from home last weekend?***
*She's been **studying hard at home all year.***

NOTE: The exceptions to this rule are verbs of motion – e.g. **go, come, arrive** – where the adverb of place tends to come before the adverb of manner.
*She went **upstairs quietly.***

---

4 Complete each sentence with one of the words given at the end of the sentence. Two possible positions for the word are shown. Only one is correct.

1 The team plays .... at home ....   (good / well)

2 No one had said much but Paul seemed .... strangely ....
(quiet / quietly)

3 The police found .... his story .... to believe.
(hard / hardly)

4   We're looking for a .... quiet .... place to stay.
    (nice / nicely)

5   The exam looked .... at first .... but I'm sure I did well.
    (tough / toughly)

6   Most of our athletes ran .... this morning ....
    (superb / superbly)

7   I'm looking for a quiet, but .... located .... flat in the
    Heansley area.   (central / centrally)

8   The forest fire spread .... incredibly ....
    (quick / quickly)

COMMUNICATIVE PRACTICE

1 Rotten apples

Look at the unfinished sentences below and the lists of adjectives and adverbs that follow
them. With another student, work out which adjective or adverb could *not* be used to
complete each sentence. Then draw a line connecting all the words which do not fit (all
the 'rotten apples'). Then draw a second line parallel to the first one. For example: (far).

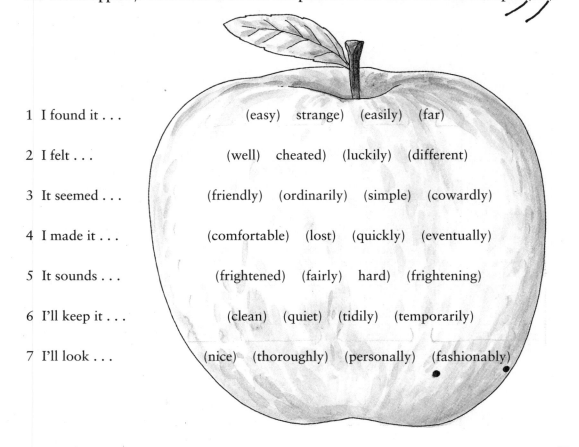

1 I found it . . .   (easy)   strange)   (easily)   (far)

2 I felt . . .   (well)   cheated)   (luckily)   (different)

3 It seemed . . .   (friendly)   (ordinarily)   (simple)   (cowardly)

4 I made it . . .   (comfortable)   (lost)   (quickly)   (eventually)

5 It sounds . . .   (frightened)   (fairly)   hard)   (frightening)

6 I'll keep it . . .   (clean)   (quiet)   (tidily)   (temporarily)

7 I'll look . . .   (nice)   (thoroughly)   (personally)   (fashionably)

2 Palm reading

Look at the diagram and the table below. The diagram shows the lines of the palm and the table shows the name and significant features of each line. Working with another student, try to work out what each line can tell you. The first one has been done for you.

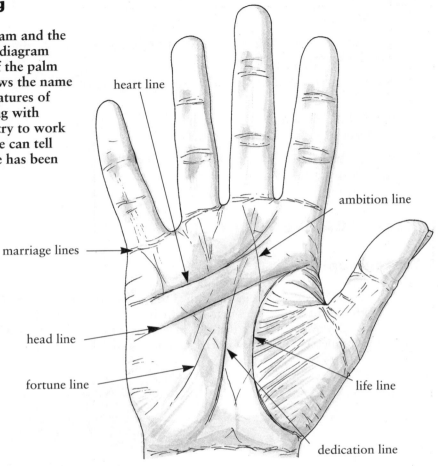

heart line

ambition line

marriage lines

head line

fortune line

life line

dedication line

Name	Significant features	
Life line	A long line A break in the line	*indicates a long and healthy life.* *points to a period serious illness.*
Dedication line	A long line . . . An unbroken line . . .	
Fortune line	The place where it begins . . .	
Head line	A long line . . .	
Marriage lines	The closeness to the heart line . . . The number of small lines . . .	
Heart line	A long curved line indicates . . . A deeply coloured line . . . The number of small lines coming from it . . .	
Ambition line	A long line . . . The place where it begins . . .	

Once you have checked your answers with your teacher, try reading each other's palms. You must read the right hand as shown in the diagram.

Example:

A: *You're going to have a long and healthy life, without being seriously ill.*
B: *Are you sure?*
A: *Yes. Look at how long your life line is – and there are no breaks in it.*

EXAM FOCUS

EXAM TIP 4

Three questions

There are three things you have to ask yourself when doing a word formation question:

a) what *part of speech* is needed in the gap?
b) will changing the word involve a *change of spelling*?
c) does a *prefix/suffix* need to be added?

1 Word formation

The word in capitals at the end of each of the following sentences can be used to form an adjective or adverb that fits suitably in the blank space. Fill each blank in this way.

Example: *The doctor said it would be **inadvisable** to continue smoking.* ADVICE

1 The waiter .... spilt some wine on the table. ACCIDENT

2 The actors clearly became more .... as the play progressed.
CONFIDENCE

3 The war made hundreds of innocent people .... HOME

4 I found the shop assistant .... rude when I took the shoes back to the shop. NECESSARY

5 The wreckage from the plane gave no clue as to what went so ....
wrong. TRAGEDY

6 It must be the wine that is making me feel .... SLEEP

7 Lying like that was a really .... thing to do. COWARD

8 If you do your homework so .... you can't possibly hope to pass the course. CARE

9 According to the opinion polls, he should win the election quite ....
EASE

10 Your idea sounds .... but will it actually work in practice?
IMPRESS

EXAM TIP 5

Supporting information

When supplying the missing word in a cloze exercise involves making decisions about vocabulary as well as grammar, be careful to look for supporting information elsewhere in the passage which will help you to work out what the word might be.

2 Cloze

Fill each of the numbered blanks in the following passage. Use only *one* word in each space.

The man who holds the record for being struck by lightning the most times is ex-park ranger, Roy Sullivan. Mr Sullivan found lightning (1) .... to avoid: he was struck by it on seven (2) .... occasions throughout his life, which were as (3) .... as 35 years apart.

The first incident in 1942 was the only one where he was not (4) .... injured – he only lost his big toenail. On all other occasions, he could quite (5) .... have lost his life. In 1972 the 'human lightning conductor of Virginia', as he was known, had his hair set on fire but was (6) .... enough to survive, only to lose all his new hair in the same way a year later. It is (7) .... to believe that he never lost his enthusiasm for outdoor hobbies and pursuits but when lightning struck for a record seventh time in 1977 he was happily fishing, (8) .... unaware that he was about to enter *The Guinness Book of Records*. On this occasion he came very (9) .... to death because of severe chest and stomach burns. Roy Sullivan died in 1983 but was not killed by lightning. He was deeply (10) .... after being rejected in love and is said to have taken his own life.

(adapted from *The Guinness Book of Records 1987*)

Unit 4 The past

Language focus: uses of the past simple, past continuous, past perfect and past perfect continuous; past tenses after special phrases

Exam focus: cloze and dialogue building questions

LEAD-IN

Read these two short passages about the rainy season in South-East Asia and then complete the task below.

Passage 1

The river was rising steadily when term ended. It was still possible to drive through the streets of Kuala Hantu, but dwellers near the river's edge had taken to the roofs and the bazaar had had to close down. Up-stream the rain thundered and soon, in time for Christmas, Kuala Hantu would resound to the whip-lashings of the frenzied sky.

(adapted from Anthony Burgess, *The Long Day Wanes*)

Passage 2

Then, on a hot afternoon, we felt a fresh breeze hitting our faces. Small waves were beginning to bump the boat. The wind had changed and the fish had begun their annual migration northward. The monsoon that had been blowing constantly from the Indian Ocean from May to September now gave way to the drier cooler monsoon from Mongolia. The rainy season was over. An excited villager remarked that now the crabs and frogs would taste better.

(adapted from Thomas O'Neill, 'The Mekong River', *National Geographic*)

Mark the events mentioned in each passage on the time lines below, as in the example.

Passage 1

before	same time	after
	a	

end of term

a) the rising of the river
b) moving to the roofs
c) the closing of the bazaar
d) rain up-stream
e) lightning in Kuala Hantu

Passage 2

before	same time	after

one hot afternoon

a) waves around the boat
b) change in the wind
c) migration of the fish
d) monsoon from the Indian Ocean
e) the villager's remark
f) tastier crabs and frogs

REFERENCE

A *The past simple*

Form

Affirmative	*Negative*
I worked, etc.	I did not (didn't) work, etc.
Question	*Short answers*
Did you work?	Yes, I did. No, I didn't.

Some verbs have an irregular affirmative form. For a complete list of these see page 146.

Use

We use the past simple tense to talk about completed actions or habits in the past. We use it when some definite point or period in time is mentioned or understood.

*My husband and I **met in the last year of school**.*
*When I was at the market **this morning** I **saw** Pat.* (it's now afternoon)
***As a child** I never **stayed up** later than nine o'clock.*

NOTE: In the last example, we could use the phrase **used to** to talk about past habit instead.

*As a child I **never used/didn't use to** stay up . . .*

B *The past continuous*

Form

Affirmative	*Negative*
I was working, etc.	I was not (wasn't) working, etc.
Question	*Short answers*
Were you working?	Yes, I was. No, I wasn't.

Uses

1 We use the past continuous tense to talk about actions in progress in the past around a particular point in time.

*I **was** probably **working** in the garden when you rang.*
*My family **was living** in Germany at the time the Berlin Wall came down.*

The actions are usually longer, rather than shorter, and we are not normally interested in when the past continuous action started or finished.

2 As well as talking about one general idea (a past action in progress) it is useful to think about the uses of the past continuous tense that are listed in the following exercise.

1 Look at the descriptions of uses in a–d and match them to each pair of example sentences in 1–4.

   a) to provide background description or detail in a story
   b) to describe actions which are interrupted
   c) to talk about temporary situations in the past
   d) to talk about two longer actions which happen at the same time

1 Sarah **was talking** to someone on the phone as I walked in.
   The film **was** just **getting** interesting when the picture went.

2 We both had friends who **were staying** in Spain that summer.
   I usually stacked the shelves but I **was working** at the check-out that week.

3 The child noticed that the man **was holding** an unusual stick.
   The rain **was beating** down outside and the children from the flat next door **were running** and **screaming** in the hallway.

4 I **was trying** to work while someone outside **was drilling**.
   The police didn't know that the murderer **was sitting** in jail accused of theft all the time they **were looking** for him.

2 Complete the story below by putting the verbs in brackets into either the past simple or past continuous tense.

A young English language student who (1) .... (spend) the summer in

Britain, (2) .... (decide) one day that he would like to visit a friend in another

town. Having just done a unit in his coursebook on 'public transport', he (3) ....

(think) it would be a good idea to take the train. He (4) .... (get) ready to

leave when he suddenly (5) .... (realise) that there was one important

phrase that the coursebook he (6) .... (use) at school had not taught him.

He (7) .... (take) out his dictionary and after a short search

(8) .... (find) the phrase 'return ticket'. Arriving at the train station, he

(9) .... (walk) boldly up to the ticket office and in his best English accent

said to the man who (10) .... (sit) at the desk: 'I'd like a return ticket,

please.' The man (11) .... (stare) at him for a moment questioningly and

then (12) .... (ask): 'Where to?' The student, who was used to his teacher

asking him such questions to check that he really (13) .... (understand) the

meaning of the words he (14) .... (use), looked confidently back at the man

and replied: 'Back here, of course.'

C *The past perfect*

Form

Affirmative	Negative
I had (I'd) worked, etc.	I had not (hadn't) worked, etc.
Question	*Short answers*
Had you worked?	Yes, I had. No, I hadn't.

Uses

1 When already talking about the past we use the past perfect to talk about an earlier past time.
   *His face was familiar. I **had met** him somewhere before.*
   *The hotel wasn't particularly good but I **had stayed** in many that were worse.*

2 We use the past perfect tense when one past action is closely connected to another to show which one happened first.
   *Wendy **hadn't left** the key so I climbed through a window.*

   This use is very common with time words and phrases such as:

when	before	after	by the time

   *Most of the guests **had left** by the time I got there.*
   *It began to rain just after the party **had started**.*

   NOTE: The past simple (not the past perfect) is used if one action is an immediate reaction to another.
   *When he **saw** the face at the window, he **fainted**.*
   *The child **stopped** crying as soon as she **caught** sight of her mother.*

D *The past perfect continuous*

Form

Affirmative	Negative
I had (I'd) been working, etc.	I had not (hadn't) been working, etc.
Question	*Short answers*
Had you been working?	Yes, I had. No, I hadn't.

Use

We use the past perfect continuous tense to talk about an action which had been in progress before another.

I'd been quietly reading the paper before the train compartment filled up.

Like the past continuous, it is used to talk about the longer, background events in a story.

I'd been visiting doctors for several years with the same complaint before it was correctly diagnosed.

E Past tenses after special phrases

The phrases below are followed by a special pattern of tenses: the past simple when there is a present focus to the sentence, and the past perfect when there is a past focus.

Present focus

It's time we went/were going home. (I think we should go.)
I wish you didn't have to go. (You have to go which makes me sad.)
I'd rather we went together. (I want us / I'd prefer to go together.)

Past focus

I wish he hadn't come. (I'm not happy that he came.)
I'd rather we hadn't stayed so late. (We stayed later than I wanted to.)
If only you hadn't left. (I'm unhappy that you left.)

3 Match sentences 1–6 to the explanations given in a–f.

1 It's time we had a holiday.	a) This one is really dirty.
2 I wish we had had more time.	b) I really wanted to stay.
3 I wish we had a few more days.	c) The campsite looks awful.
4 I'd rather we stayed in a hotel.	d) It was very expensive.
5 If only we'd found a better hotel.	e) I'd really like to see some more sights.
6 I'd rather we hadn't stayed so long.	f) We deserve a break.

4 Look at the following pairs of sentences and discuss the possible differences in meaning with another student.

Example:

a) When we got to the corner, Matthew waited.
   This means: 'Matthew was with us and when we got to the corner he stopped.'

b) When we got to the corner, Matthew was waiting.
   This means: 'Matthew was not with us. When we got to the corner he was there waiting for us.'

1 a) I was told that my friends hadn't waited for me.
  b) I was told that my friends hadn't been waiting for me.

2 a) The children went to bed when their parents got home.
  b) The children had gone to bed when their parents got home.

3 a) Mary didn't drive so she didn't have a car.
   b) Mary hadn't driven so she didn't have a car.

4 a) I argued with my wife when her parents came.
   b) I was arguing with my wife when her parents came.

5 a) Lucy hadn't been sleeping well at all before the interview.
   b) Lucy didn't sleep well at all before the interview.

6 a) I'd rather you didn't come with us.
   b) I'd rather you hadn't come with us.

COMMUNICATIVE PRACTICE

1 Short story bingo

Think of two *unusual* or *amusing* things that have happened to you in the past and think of how you can tell these stories. Look at the words in the bingo boxes below to help you remember, although you must not use these words in telling your short stories.

Now think about some of the vocabulary you will need to tell your stories.

Take it in turns to tell your stories to the class.

Below are two bingo cards. You will be given *one* of them to mark as your card. As you listen to the stories from other members of the class put an X in the box on your card if you hear an event or incident in a story that could be described by one of the phrases.

When you have a horizontal, vertical or diagonal line of three phrases, shout 'Bingo!'. You will then have to explain to the rest of the class which three incidents or events match the phrases you have marked.

The first person to get two correct lines is the winner.

A

Sweet revenge	Embarrassing moment	Strange coincidence
The wrong moment	Unexpected surprise	Unusual request
Lucky escape	Chance meeting	Misunderstanding

B

A total stranger	A stroke of good luck	Unique opportunity
Love at first sight	Lucky escape	A familiar face
Strange coincidence	Something peculiar	Chance meeting

2 Whose story?

Work with two other students. In your group decide upon a story to tell the rest of the class. The story has to be about something that has happened to *one* member of the group and it must be *true*.

When you have decided on a story, divide it up so that one person tells the beginning, another person the middle and the third person the end. Make sure every member of the group has all the facts they need to tell their part of the story.

When telling the story to the rest of the class, each member of the group must tell it as though it were his/her story (using the personal pronouns and possessive adjectives *I, we, my, our*, etc.). Tell the story as if you were really involved in what happened and try and give your listeners:

- the background situation / setting;
- important descriptive information about the characters / events;
- a sense of anticipation in waiting for the end.

After each story the rest of the class can ask *two* questions to any member of the group about the story. The rest of the class will then have to guess whose story it was.

EXAM FOCUS

1 Cloze

Fill each of the numbered blanks in the following passage. Use only *one* word in each space.

At 15,000 feet on the Plateau of Tibet in China there was nowhere to hide. The snow flew like arrows. The Tibetan herder Meiga, who (1) .... forcing his horse through the storm, searched in vain for shelter. When visibility dropped to near zero all we could do (2) .... stop and bunch up the horses. Huddled together, heads bowed, we (3) .... the storm beat on us.

My goal was to travel the length of the Mekong, the world's twelfth longest river. To reach this place, I (4) .... travelled a thousand miles by old army jeep from Xining. Now, as we sheltered behind our horses, I wondered if we (5) .... have to turn back. Then the storm lifted, as suddenly as it had (6) .... , leaving a bruised grey sky.

We rode another hour before coming to a solitary, cone-shaped hill. 'The holy mountain,' Meiga said. He reached into a saddlebag and (7) .... out a stack of coloured papers printed with Buddhist scripture. He shouted and flung the prayers high into the air and watched happily as the wind (8) .... them away.

We rode behind the mountain and found a sheet of ice some 300 yards long – shaped like an hourglass. Crouching down on the frozen surface, I (9) .... hear below a trickle of water. It was the beginning notes of the Mekong. Mike and I had (10) .... , as far as I can discover, the first Western journalists to hear them.

(adapted from Thomas O'Neill, 'The Mekong River', *National Geographic*)

2 Dialogue building

Complete the numbered gaps in the following imaginary interview with the journalist who travelled the length of the Mekong river.

Interviewer: Tom. You and your photographer, Mike Yamashita, recently travelled the length of Asia's mighty Mekong river.

Journalist: That's right.

Interviewer: (1) .... before?

Journalist: It's hard to say, but I'm pretty sure we were the first Western journalists to do so.

Interviewer: (2) .... all the way?

Journalist: No, we couldn't always get permission to use a boat so we often rented horses or donkeys. Getting permission and visas to visit places was actually our biggest problem.

Interviewer: (3) .... ?

Journalist: Almost five months altogether because we started from the river's source in Tibet.

Interviewer: And (4) .... ?

Journalist: All six that are home to the river: China, Burma, Laos, Thailand, Cambodia and Vietnam.

Interviewer: What (5) .... ?

Journalist: It was all interesting. There was never a dull moment. But what fascinated me the most were the floating homes in Vietnam under which people keep and breed huge catfish.

Interviewer: You mean . . . actually under the floor?

Journalist: Yes, that's right.

Interviewer: And did you experience the famous monsoon season?

Journalist: Not really, by the time we started (6) ....

Interviewer: So (7) .... ?

Journalist: Very good, except for the snow storms in the Tibetan mountains right at the start of the trip when I almost felt like giving up.

Interviewer: (8) .... like doing that?

Journalist: Yes, the only time. Once you start on a river like the Mekong, it just carries you with it.

Unit 5 Articles and determiners

Language focus: use of articles and determiners with countable and uncountable nouns
Exam focus: multiple-choice and telegramese questions

LEAD-IN

1 With another student, look at the words in the box below and decide whether they are likely to be used as *countable* nouns (with a plural form) or *uncountable* nouns (without a plural form). Write 'c' or 'un' next to each noun. Check your answers with another pair of students.

history	banking	world	gold bar	foreign currency
pottery	document	door	information	collection

2 The words and phrases in bold print in the text below are examples of how articles are used in English. Read the text and complete the 'Use of articles' table by matching at least one example to each rule.

The Bank of England Museum

(1) **The museum** is housed within the Bank of England itself, right at the heart of the City of London. It traces (2) **the history** of the Bank from its foundation by Royal Charter in 1694 to (3) t**he high-tech world** of (4) **modern banking**.

There are (5) **gold bars** dating from (6) **ancient times** to the modern market bar, coins and (7) **a unique collection** of banknotes, as well as many other items you might not expect to find – such as (8) **the Roman pottery and mosaics** uncovered when the Bank was rebuilt in the 1930s. On display are (9) **documents** relating to the Duchess of Marlborough and George Washington, both former customers of the Bank.

The Bank Stock Office, (10) **a late eighteenth-century banking hall** designed by the great English architect Sir John Soane, has been reconstructed and (11) **interactive videos** give visitors the opportunity of looking behind (12) **the doors** of the nation's central bank. (13) **Live news** and information about securities and (14) **foreign currency** is given at a dealing desk, which is identical to those in daily use in the Bank, and visitors can imagine themselves in the world of high finance.

(adapted from *Bank of England Museum: A Souvenir Guide*)

Use of articles

The

<table>
<tr><td>1 The is used with all nouns to talk about particular things when we say which one/ones we mean.
Examples: .... 2 ....</td></tr>
<tr><td>2 The is used with all nouns when the reader already knows the particular thing we are talking about, i.e. it has been mentioned before.
Example: ....</td></tr>
</table>

A / an

<table>
<tr><td>1 A / an is used with countable nouns when something is mentioned for the first time, when we mean '(there is) one'.
Example: ....</td></tr>
<tr><td>2 A / an is used with countable nouns to say what something or someone is, e.g. giving a definition of something, or saying what someone's profession is.
Example: ....</td></tr>
</table>

No article

<table>
<tr><td>1 No article is used with plural and uncountable nouns when we are talking about things in general, when we mean 'all'.
Examples: ....</td></tr>
<tr><td>2 No article is used with plural and uncountable nouns when something is mentioned in the text for the first time, when we mean '(there is / are) some'.
Examples: ....</td></tr>
</table>

REFERENCE

1 Discuss with another student whether the following statements are true or false. Then check your answers by reading Sections A and B below.

   1 A singular countable noun, e.g. **boy**, can be used with no article.
   2 The word **news** is used with a singular verb form.
   3 In the following sentence both alternatives are grammatically correct: *I think I need a coffee / some coffee.*
   4 We can talk about *a piece of advice* and *a piece of equipment.*

A *Countable nouns*

<table>
<tr><td>1 Countable nouns are those that have both a plural and singular form: things / persons that we can count.
a policeman   two policemen   an armchair   several armchairs</td></tr>
</table>

2 Singular countable nouns *must* be used with an article or similar word.

The headmaster needs a volunteer to help.
Every volunteer is welcome.

3 Plural countable nouns can be used with no article or with **some** or **any**.

Prices are unusually high this year.
Some books have gone missing from the library.
Aren't there any cheaper shoes left?

B Uncountable nouns

1 Uncountable nouns do not have a plural form and are always used with a singular form of the verb.

The weather has been really terrible lately.
The information isn't complete.

2 Uncountable nouns cannot be used with the indefinite article (**a / an**). They can be used with **some** and **any** or **no article**.

There isn't any milk left.
Bread and water are in short supply.

3 Sometimes, however, we do wish to talk about 'quantity' with uncountable nouns and then we have to use a special structure:

I need a bar of soap. (not 'a soap')
My family eats four loaves of bread a day. (not 'four breads')

4 The nouns below are uncountable in English but tend to be countable in other languages. All the nouns in bold print can be used with the phrase **a piece of**.

An important piece of equipment is missing.

advice	applause	damage	**equipment**	**evidence**	**furniture**	hair
harm	**information**	**knowledge**	lightning	**luggage**	**news**
progress	proof	**research**	thunder	trouble	

5 Some nouns can be both countable and uncountable, e.g. materials and substances, depending on how we use them:

coffee	tea	beer	sugar	glass	paper	skin

Can I have a coffee? (a cup of . . .)
We've run out of coffee.

2 Complete each sentence below with a word from the box. (You won't need all the words.)

skin	assistant	idea	beer	equipment
news	tool	advice	customer	reports

1 You're working too hard. You need a reliable ....

2 Haven't you got rough .... ?

3 I'm afraid we can't serve .... before six o'clock.

4 .... of the situation in Africa get worse each day.

5 You need a different .... to do the job properly.

6 Contact an employment agency to get an .... about how much extra staff will cost.

7 I've heard a piece of .... that might interest you.

8 You can't expect to satisfy every .... all the time.

3 Complete the sentences below by choosing the correct alternative of the two given in brackets. Then check your answers by reading through Sections C and D.

(The line —— means 'no article'.)

1 The book contained very .... useful information.   (few / little)

2 .... French have a great football team at the moment.   (—— / The)

3 Did Beethoven ever compose for .... guitar?   (a / the)

4 .... prices fell during the second half of the year.   (Most / Less)

5 I'm afraid there isn't really .... advice I can give.   (much / another)

6 .... cigarettes aren't as popular as they used to be.   (—— / The)

C *Articles*

1 The is used with all nouns:

   a when the listener/reader already knows the person / thing we are talking about.
   *I can't give you **the five pounds** back.*

   b when we say exactly which person / thing we mean.
   ***The glass you just gave me** is cracked.*
   ***The** famous actress **Cher** was there.*

   c when there is only one of the thing we are talking about.
   ***The environment** is in great danger.*

   d and with these categories of noun to talk about the thing in general:
   musical instruments   animals   plants   inventions   nationalities.
   *I play **the guitar** quite well.*
   ***The Spanish** make the best salads.*

2 A / an is used with singular countable nouns:

   a when mentioning something / someone for the first time.
   *The museum also has **a rare sculpture**.*

   b to say what someone / something is.
   *My uncle is **a teacher**.*

c to talk about a person / thing in general.
A car is no longer considered a luxury.

3 **No article** is used with plural and uncountable nouns:

a when we mention the thing / things for the first time.
Food and drinks will be served later.

b when we talk about the thing / things in general.
Life in the developing world is tough.
Modern cars last five to ten ye.ars.

D Determiners

1 The following determiners are all used with singular countable nouns. Those in bold print can *only* be used with singular countable nouns.

a / an	**another**	any	**each**	**either**	**every**	**neither**	no

Every member was given a free pass.

2 The following determiners are all used with plural countable nouns. Those in bold print can *only* be used with plural countable nouns.

all	any	**both**	enough	**few**	**fewer**	**many**
more	most	no	**other**	**several**	some	

Several guests arrived after the speeches.

3 The following determiners are all used with uncountable nouns. Those in bold print can *only* be used with uncountable nouns.

all	any	enough	**less**	**little**	more	most	**much**	no	some

*The speakers were given **very little** time.*

4 **Many** is used with plural countable nouns, **much** with uncountable nouns.
*There aren't **many lakes** in Greece.*
*How **much aid** had already reached the area?*

But they are only used in questions and negative statements. In affirmative statements we use **a lot of**.
A lot of equipment was damaged by the fire.

5 **Little / a little** are used with uncountable nouns.
Little money has been given so far. (not much)
A little money would help a lot. (some)

6 **Few / a few** are used with plural countable nouns.
*Very **few countries** grow all their own food.* (not many)
*A **few people** have already been informed.* (some)

COMMUNICATIVE PRACTICE

1 Which one fits?

With another student look at the types of food and drink in the box and decide which words are used as uncountable nouns and which ones as countable nouns when talking about the food and drink in general.

Example: *Potato is a countable noun.*

| potato | cheese | chocolate | tea | egg | coffee |

Write the words in the table below. (The first one has been done for you.)

Now decide which one of these types of food and drink fits all the categories below. There is *only one* right answer.

	Can affect your sleep	Can harm your teeth	Can make you more excitable or alert	It/its main ingredient comes from the southern hemisphere	Can be counted like soap
potatoes					
....					
....					
....					
....					
....					

2 What's missing?

Look at the cartoons. Something is missing from each one. With another student read the caption that goes with each cartoon and try and work out what the missing parts of the picture might be.

1

'OK, kids, bedtime.'

2

'How's the article on recycling going?'

3

4

5

'Oh, thank God – I hate to drink alone!'

6

'I'm sorry, but I think I've forgotten your name.'

EXAM FOCUS

1 Multiple-choice

In the sentences below decide whether the noun you are given or are looking for is countable (circle 'c') or uncountable (circle 'un').

Then choose the word or phrase which best completes each sentence by circling the letter A, B, C or D.

1 Our old teacher has found an excellent .... abroad.   c / un
   A employment   B work   C post   D staffing

2 The forecast says we can expect .... nasty weather.   c / un
   A several   B a   C a few   D some

3 .... boy will admit that he caused all the damage.   c / un
   A Neither   B Both   C None   D Several

4 You're travelling with much less .... than usual.   c / un
   A suitcases   B luggage   C handbag   D packages

5 More .... into this drug is planned for next year.   c / un
   A investigation   B research   C experiment   D test

6 I had no idea that parking would prove so .... trouble.   c / un
   A great   B much   C many   D few

7 The company had to hire a van to move .... furniture.   c / un
   A those   B a   C a little   D another

8 Fighting at the nightclub caused several serious ....   c / un
   A injuries   B wound   C damages   D breakage

9 One important .... about the crime had been overlooked.   c / un
   A information   B detail   C evidence   D knowledge

10 There was not enough .... for four in the new flat.   c / un
   A room   B place   C area   D measurement

EXAM TIP 7

It's all part of a letter

One of the main things you have to do in a 'telegramese' question is to add words like determiners and articles to make each line read like a continuous sentence. Remember, however, to read each line as part of the whole letter because use of articles / no article, etc. can depend on whether the person / thing has already been mentioned.

2 Telegramese

Make all the changes and additions necessary to produce, from the following sets of words and phrases, sentences which together make a complete letter. Write each sentence in the space provided.

Bank of England Museum,
London

5th April 1994

The Director,
Clarke's Language Institute,
London

Dear Mrs Porter,

1 Thank you / letter / enquiring / visit / Bank of England Museum.

....

2 We be happy / arrange visit / for group of students / mentioned / your letter.

....

3 I suggest / visit include / film show about / Bank's history, follow / brief tour.

....

4 There then be / opportunity for students / use / some of latest banking equipment / in use / Bank today.

....

5 If students be interested, / can also use / interactive videos in Museum / find information / careers / banking.

....

6 Please find enclosed / copies / leaflets about Museum / help you / prepare students / before visit.

....

7 We organise / similar visits / in the past / language students / be great success.

....

8 We look forward / meet you / 20th April.

....

Yours sincerely,

Malcolm Campbell
Public Relations Officer

Unit 6 Dependent prepositions

Language focus: dependent prepositions after adjectives and verbs; dependent prepositions and sentence patterns

Exam focus: cloze and multiple-choice questions

LEAD-IN

1 Albert is a complex person with many different characteristics. These are shown in the maze of his mind below, with positive characteristics on the left and negative ones on the right. However, the prepositions in these descriptions have all been missed out, and where they are missing there are gaps in the walls of the maze.

Working in a group, start in the middle of the maze and try to get out through the positive side by choosing the correct prepositions. For example, 'good at hiding feelings' will allow you to go through that gap. You only need to go through one gap in each wall.

Write down the prepositions you choose, and when you have found a way out, tell your teacher. If your prepositions are all correct, you have won. If not, you must wait to try again until another group has checked their prepositions with the teacher.

When one group has won, do the same with the negative side of the maze.

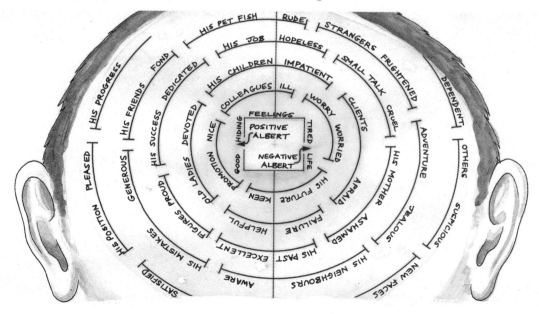

2 Look back at the maze and write in the box below any adjectives to do with *ability* (how good/bad someone is).

Look back at the maze and write in the box below any adjectives to do with *people's behaviour towards things / other people.*

Which preposition do these adjectives take?

REFERENCE

A *Dependent prepositions after adjectives*

Complete the second example in each box so that it is a true statement about yourself.

1 At is used after adjectives of ability:

awful   bad   excellent   good   great   terrible   useless

*My son's not so **good at** maths.*
I'm really

....

2 To and **of** are used with adjectives describing behaviour:

cruel   friendly   helpful   kind   nasty   nice   offensive   polite   rude

To refers to the object of the action:

*She was **rude to** her father.*
.... *to me.*

Of in phrases with an impersonal subject (**it/that**):

*It/that was really **kind of** you.*

3 About and **with** are used with adjectives describing reactions to people/events:

concerned   embarrassed   positive   worried   **about** something / someone

*Our teacher is **concerned about** our slow progress.*

....

bored   disgusted   impressed   patient   **with** somebody / something

*He's very **patient with** the children.*

....

angry   annoyed   furious   upset   **with** somebody / **about** something

*Eva got **upset with** me for not calling.*

....

disappointed   happy   pleased   **with** somebody / **about** an event / **with** a situation

*I'm not **pleased with** the way my work is going.*

*He's very **happy about** being selected to play on Saturday.*

I'm really not ....

---

4 **Of** is used with certain adjectives describing more lasting feelings:

afraid   ashamed   fond   frightened   jealous   suspicious   tired   wary

*Who's the child so **afraid of**?*

I've never ....

---

5 NOTE: Sometimes words such as **frightened, worried, upset** and **embarrassed** are used as past participle forms. When used in a passive construction they will be followed by the preposition **by**.

*My cousin is **frightened of** spiders.* (always)

*My cousin was **frightened by** a spider running across the floor.* (this spider frightened him)

B *Dependent prepositions after verbs*

Read the information in the boxes below and complete the second sentence in each box to make a true statement about you and the FCE exam. This could be about preparing for or sitting the exam, or about getting the results.

---

1 **At** is used after certain verbs to show the object of attention:

aim   fire   laugh   look   point   scream   shout   smile   stare
throw   whistle   yell

*Our neighbour often **stares at** me through the window.*

....

---

2 **For** is used after certain verbs to introduce the purpose of the action:

apologise   hope   look   long   pray   search   wait

*We're **hoping for** better weather this time.*

It is also used with certain transitive verbs this way:

ask   blame   forgive   prepare

*The rest of the team **blamed me for** the mistake.*

*She's never **forgiven me for** not telling her.*

....

---

3 **About** is used after certain verbs of speech to introduce the topic:

ask   complain   explain   lie   talk   tell   warn   wonder   write

*Was the driver **lying about** his address?*

....

4 **To** is used after certain verbs of speech to introduce other people involved:

apologise   explain   listen   speak   suggest   talk   write

*Has your boss **apologised to** you yet?*

....

5 **On** is used after certain verbs to introduce the object of the action:

check   concentrate   count   depend   insist   rely

*We can't **rely on** my parents coming to get us.*

In writing the essays ....

6 **From** is used after certain verbs which have the meaning of stopping something:

discourage   dissuade   keep   prevent   stop

*The guards **prevented me from** leaving the room.*

Nothing ....

C Dependent prepositions and sentence patterns

1 After a dependent preposition we use an **-ing** verb form.

*My brother is afraid **of** people **laughing** at him.*
*Aren't our neighbours talking **about moving** abroad?*

But with some adjectives we can drop the preposition and use an infinitive instead.

*She's **afraid to go** out alone.*

We also use an infinitive when an adjective is used with **too**.

*The child was **too embarrassed to** perform.*

2 The object pronoun relating to a following verb comes between the dependent preposition and the **-ing** form.

*Aren't you bored **with him talking** about himself?*

3 The negatives **not** and **never** also come between the dependent preposition and the **-ing** form.

*The patient apologised **for not being** on time.*

4 When **to** is a dependent preposition it is followed by an **-ing** form as in the following words / phrases:

look forward to	be opposed to	get/be used to	dedicated to
prefer . . . to	admit to	object to	

*I **prefer getting** up early **to staying** on late at work.*
*My son's never really been **dedicated to becoming** a doctor.*

(See Unit 8 for dependent prepositions and relative clauses.)

1 Match the beginnings of the questions on the left to the ends of the questions on the right.

1 Don't you think we should complain	a) to see anyone?
2 Why don't you explain	b) you for what happened?
3 Shouldn't you concentrate	c) for the delay?
4 Won't she be too upset	d) it to her?
5 Aren't you tired	e) on getting better, rather than work?
6 Didn't Kim apologise	f) with your results?
7 Does Keith blame	g) of not having any free time?
8 Aren't you pleased	h) to them about having to wait?
9 Hasn't he already asked	i) to us doing overtime?
10 Do you think they'll object	j) you for some money?

COMMUNICATIVE PRACTICE

1 How did you feel?

Imagine yourself in two of the situations below. Write about how you felt in each one using at least two or three of the adjectives from the Lead-in and Reference sections.

Example: (1) *It was really wrong of him to do that. I felt so embarrassed about it at the time and really annoyed with him afterwards. He was playing with people's feelings and being cruel to both of us.*

1 A friend arranged a blind date for you with someone twice (or half) your age.
2 You were caught looking at someone else's answer paper during an exam.
3 On a walk through a forest you got separated from the rest of the group.
4 In a busy department store you were wrongly accused of shoplifting by a store detective.
5 Your friends laughed at you when you told them that you had applied for a much better job.
6 You went out one night with a group of friends and you ended up buying most of the drinks.
7 You went to see your boss about a personal problem and he/she said that he/she didn't have time to discuss it.
8 You were elected student of the year by teachers and had to give a speech to the whole school.

Then show your descriptions to two other students and see if they can guess which situations you have written about. Do not describe what happened, only how people reacted and how you felt.

Discuss how the two other students in your group felt in their imaginary situations. Would you feel the same way?

2 A murder mystery

Lady Stephanie Chattsworth died from kissing a letter written with poisoned ink. Read the information below about Lady Stephanie and the people suspected of her murder. Then, using the verbs on the arrows below, discuss with another student how the characters felt about each other and who might have murdered Lady Stephanie.

For example, with *forgave* on the arrow from Lord Chattsworth to Lady Stephanie you could say, 'Lord Chattsworth forgave his wife for her affair with the butler.'

Lady Stephanie Chattsworth was a very attractive forty-year-old woman. She was very fond of her husband, Lord Chattsworth, but fell madly in love with the butler at Chattsworth Manor, Craig Walker. She died after kissing the poisoned picture of a red rose.

forgave

explained

was convinced   disapproved

depended   was lying

objected   was preventing

blamed   hated

Lord Chattsworth is a seventy-year-old millionaire. He was deeply upset by his wife's affair with the butler, Craig Walker, and has sacked Mr Walker.

Suzanne Chattsworth is Lord Chattsworth's only daughter. Her mother, the first Lady Chattsworth, died three years ago, and she did not want her father to marry again. She loves the life of high society and spends all her time, and a lot of money, on going to parties.

was relying

longed

Craig Walker is a handsome young man who had never worked as a butler before coming to Chattsworth Manor. It was Lord Chattsworth's daughter, Suzanne, who encouraged her father to employ him. Now he has lost his job he regrets the affair with Stephanie.

EXAM FOCUS

1 Cloze

a **Fill each of the numbered blanks in the following passage. Use only *one* preposition in each space.**

It was getting very late and she was worried (1) .... Steve. He had told her

something (2) .... a man he would have to wait (3) .... but had rushed

out of the door before she could ask any more. Steve was someone that you could usually

rely (4) .... to be frank and honest but he had changed of late and Annie objected

(5) .... him being so secretive. Something or someone was stopping him

(6) .... coming clean. She was tired (7) .... all the pretence and promised

herself that she would ask him (8) .... a thorough explanation as soon as he walked

through the door.

b **Fill each of the numbered blanks in the following passage. Use only *one* word in each space. You will need to use various types of words (verbs, prepositions, negatives, etc.) but all the missing words relate in some way to the grammar covered in this unit.**

Thais are naturally friendly people and will want to make you feel at home. There are a few

basic rules you should observe, however. Do not point your feet directly (1) .... a

Thai – it is deeply offensive (2) .... them. Always dress discreetly in a *wat* [temple]

and remember that you will not be forgiven lightly for (3) .... taking off your shoes.

Thais are now (4) .... to seeing tourists bathe topless but nude bathing is definitely

unacceptable. Thais greet each other (5) .... a palms-together gesture; if you do

likewise you will give considerable pleasure. Thais are curious people, so will ask you

questions that westerners would not normally ask – (6) .... your salary, for example.

Do not be offended (7) .... this. It is normal to bargain in Thailand and Thais will not

get upset about you (8) .... for money off – about 15–20 per cent. Lastly, enjoy

yourself, that's a very Thai thing to do!

(adapted from Christine Osborne, *Essential Thailand*)

EXAM TIP 8

Three can't be right

The students that do the multiple-choice question the most successfully are the ones who eliminate the three wrong answers rather than going straight for the one they think is right. In questions involving dependent prepositions try and work out what preposition or alternative structure (infinitive, etc.) all four options take before deciding which one is right.

2 Multiple-choice

Choose the word or phrase which best completes each sentence by circling A, B, C or D.

Example: They tried to .... me from taking the exam.

A blame   B (prevent)   C avoid   D refuse
~~for~~   ~~in~~   ~~to do~~

1   I don't think you can .... on him being there to meet you.
     A rely   B expect   C hope   D dependent

2   The new owners were not .... about all the repairs they had to do to the house.
     A satisfied   B worried   C wary   D prepared

3   It was really rude .... you to use his nickname.
     A of   B for   C to   D from

4   Isn't anyone going to admit .... this mess?
     A to cause   B of causing   C to causing   D have caused

5   The players were not as thoroughly prepared .... the match as they should have been.
     A for   B about   C with   D on

6   We've .... you about being late for class before, haven't we?
     A warned   B discouraged   C mentioned   D explained

7   It was difficult at first but I'm .... to not going to work every day now.
     A pleased   B grateful   C relieved   D used

8   The landlady is always .... at them about the rent.
     A complaining   B shouting   C asking   D arguing

9   My cousin still hasn't .... for not coming to the party.
     A apologised   B explained   C excused   D forgiven

10 My friend was so .... about having to speak in front of all those people.
     A bored   B embarrassed   C tired   D useless

Unit 7 The present perfect simple and continuous tenses

> *Language focus:* uses of the present perfect simple tense; contrast with the past simple tense; uses of the present perfect continuous tense
>
> *Exam focus:* transformation and telegramese questions

LEAD-IN

1 The texts below show three different uses of the present perfect simple tense. Read the texts and note the circled perfect tenses. Then look at the four statements which follow. Three of them accurately describe the use of the perfect tense in the texts; one is false. Tick the three true statements for each use.

Use 1

> **THE PARENTS of a teenager who has stolen 400 cars last night pleaded for him to be given a tougher sentence if he does it once more.**
>
> They fear he might kill someone if he carries on with his life of crime, and say locking him up is the only way to stop him.
>
> The 15-year-old tearaway – who has so far taken cars worth more than £3 million – is due to be released in a few weeks after serving half his youth custody term.

(from the *Daily Mail*)

The present perfect simple tense is used here to talk about

A a situation which began in the past.
B a situation which continues up to the present.
C a situation which finished some time ago.
D a period of time rather than a specific point in time.

Use 2

The present perfect simple tense is used here to talk about

A a recent past action.
B exactly when the action happened.
C an action the speaker/writer believes to be news.
D a past action which has some present effect or result.

58

Use 3

Rosamond Richardson is the author of several books, and presenter of BBC TV's 'Discovering Patchwork' and co-presenter of BBC TV's 'Discovering Hedgerows'. (She has also done) a short cookery series for BBC East and a series on the uses of herbs for Anglia Television. (She has been) a regular contributor to BBC Radio Cambridgeshire.

(from Rosamund Richardson, *Vegetarian Meals*)

The present perfect simple tense is used here to talk about

A an action/event which has finished.
B exactly when the action happened. ✗
C an action which happened at some time before now.
D past experience connected to what we are talking about now.

2 **From what you have seen in Task 1, which two of these three statements are true of all uses of the present perfect simple tense?**

1 The present perfect simple can only be used to talk about the recent past.
2 The present perfect simple is not used to talk about exactly when a past event happened.
3 The present perfect simple is used to talk about past events which have some connection with the present.

REFERENCE

A *The present perfect simple*

Form

Affirmative	Negative
I have (I've) decided, etc.	I have not (haven't) decided, etc.

Question	Short answers
Have you decided?	Yes, I have. No, I haven't.

Uses

1 The present perfect simple is used to talk about an action which began in the past and continues up to the present.
I've had this pain in my back all week.
The resort has changed a lot in recent years.
It hasn't rained here for weeks.

The time expressions in box 1 are commonly used with this meaning of the present perfect simple.

Box 1

all (day)	for ages	for (two) years	How long . . . ?	lately	so far
over the (past few weeks)	recently	since (Tuesday)	up to now		

2 For / since / ago

For and **since** are used to talk about the time between the start of a situation and now. The situation is one that continues up to the moment of speaking / writing.

For is used to talk about the length or period of time, i.e. the number of hours / days. **Since** is used to talk about the period of time from the point at which it began.

Ago is used to talk about the time at which a situation began in the past. The past simple is used.

Example:

A: *Your fax arrived **two days ago**.*
B: *You mean that you've had it **for two days** and haven't replied?*
A: *I'm sorry, but I haven't been to the office **since Monday** and I've only just seen it.*

1 Complete the following sentences with either the present perfect simple or the past simple so that they are true about yourself.

1 I have lived ....

2 ....recently.

3 I've not been ....

4 .... for a long time.

5 .... some time ago.

3 The present perfect simple is used when a past action has some present effect or result.
*My watch **has stopped**.* (It might be later than we think.)
***Has** anyone **seen** my car keys?* (If you have, I can leave.)

NOTE: If we use a definite past time expression, as in box 2, the past simple tense must be used as there is no longer any idea of present effect. (See Unit 4 for more information about the past simple.)

Box 2

(hours) ago	at (six)	before (Tuesday)	during (the holiday)	earlier
in (May)	last (week)	on (Monday)	the other day	this (morning)

Compare the two responses in these two dialogues:

A: *I've lost my wallet.*
B: *Don't panic. It must be here somewhere.*

B: *Have you had a good day?*
A: *No, I lost my wallet this morning.*

4 We use the present perfect simple to talk about things that have or haven't happened at some time before the time of speaking / writing but we do not say exactly when. ✗

Has anyone in the class been to the museum before?
I've passed my driving test but I'm waiting for my licence.

The time expressions in box 3 are commonly used with this meaning of the present perfect simple.

Box 3

mid-position adverbs: already   always   ever   never   still
end-position adverbs / adverbial phrases: before   several times   yet

NOTE: **Still** is rather unusual in that it can also come before the whole verb phrase.

2 Put the words in the jumbled sentences below into the correct order. Think carefully about the position of the time adverb.

1 their / once / has / before / invaded / army

....

2 teacher / has / our / not / history / taught / always

....

3 you / been / the / to / have / yet / bank / ?

....

4 still / has / postman / not / the / come

....

5 they / never / been / trouble / have / before / in

....

6 police / have / the / already / not / twice / here / been / ?

....

B *The present perfect continuous*

Form

Affirmative
I have (I've) been working, etc.

Negative
I have not (haven't) been working, etc.

Question
Have you been working?

Short answers
Yes, I have. No, I haven't.

Uses

The uses of the present perfect continuous are best seen in comparison with the uses of the present perfect simple.

Present perfect continuous	Present perfect simple
Using the present perfect continuous may mean that the action is not finished. *We've been painting the house but still have a lot to do.*	The present perfect simple is used when the action or situation is finished. *We've painted the whole house both inside and out.*
The present perfect continuous is used to talk about the length of time an activity has been in progress. *How long have you been teaching?*	The present perfect simple is used to talk about the result of an activity, e.g. when talking about quantities or distances. *How many schools have you taught in?*
The present perfect continuous is used to talk about temporary situations. *The shop hasn't been making any money recently.*	The present perfect simple is used to talk about situations that are long-lasting or permanent. *The shop has never made any money.*
The present perfect continuous is often used when the effects of an action are still visible. *Look. It's been raining*	The present perfect simple is used to talk about the start or ending of an action. *Has it stopped raining yet?*

NOTE: The present perfect continuous is often used with the time adverbs in box 1 but *never* with those in boxes 2 and 3.

3 Complete the following short dialogues with the questions which produced B's responses.

1 A: How long .... ?

    B: Since last month at this school and two years at an English language college in Japan before that.

2 A: How much .... ?

    B: About forty-five pounds so far, but I've still got quite a bit left.

3 A: What have .... ?

    B: Mending the car again. That's why I look such a mess.

4 A: .... Don yet?

   B: Yes, I saw him this morning. He looks fine.

5 A: .... here all your life?

   B: No. I moved here about four years ago.

6 A: Have you .... ?

   B: No, not long. I had my first cigarette when I was eighteen.

COMMUNICATIVE PRACTICE

1 Messages around the house

Look at the picture of the house below and read the three messages. Where do you think they were left? Mark the places on the picture.

Why are present perfect tenses used in messages like this?

Now write a similar message about a particular object in the picture of the house but do not name it. Read your message and get the rest of the class to guess what it is.

2 Since then

Make notes about yourself four years ago under the various headings in the table below.

	Four years ago	*Since then*
Address:		
Appearance:		
Holidays:		
Hobbies:		
Taste in music:		
Ambitions:		
Worries:		

Ask another student questions about the information in their box to find out more about them four years ago and since then.

Example:

A: *Where did you go on holiday four years ago?*
B: *I went to Spain with my family.*
A: *Have you been back there since then?*
B: *Yes, we've been going every year since then but we always go to a different resort.*

Then tell another pair of students about your partner.

3 Three in a row

Read the sentences below and, with another student, complete each one with three adverbs or adverbial phrases from the grid. Find three that occur in a horizontal, vertical or diagonal row.

all month	all week	just	already	recently
the other day	yet	for ages	ever	several times
before Christmas	before	in May	lately	twice
during the lesson	this week	last	still	never

Example: *Has he done the cleaning before ?*
                               yet / before / this week

1 Our neighbours have .... moved in next door.

2 I saw the teacher really lose his temper ....

3 That student .... came to class after her skiing accident.

4 We've been having problems with our car ....

5 Our boss has had the car repaired ....

EXAM FOCUS

1 Transformation

a Finish each of the following sentences in such a way that it means the same as the sentence printed before it. In the first half of the question the key parts of the sentence that need to be changed have been highlighted for you with bold print. In the second half you are on your own.

Example: He **started** working with us three months **ago**.
He has been working for us for three months.

1 I have**n't** been here **before**.

It's the first time ....

2 **It's** ages **since** my sister **was last** here.

My sister hasn't ....

3 My father **began** smoking **when** he was eighteen.

My father has ....

4 **The last time** I **saw** her **was at** Peter's party.

I haven't ....

5 When did he start playing for United?

How long ....

6 I haven't spoken to her for two weeks.

The last time ....

7 He fell ill on Friday morning.

He has ....

b Decide which 'cues' in the box will help you to rewrite the sentences below. First match the 'cues' to the sentences and then rewrite the sentences using the cues.

a) It hasn't b) He became c) He has been d) When e) He's never f) It has been

1 He began work on the book two months ago.

....

2 He hasn't had a holiday for years.

....

3 It's the first time he has failed an exam.

....

4 The last time it rained here was in May.

....

5 He has been President for six months now.

....

6 How long have they been married?

....

EXAM TIP 9

The whole, not the parts

Don't think of the telegramese question as ten separate sentences. All the sentences together make a whole letter and reading them as such will help you to work out what changes you have to make. The two basic things you have to do in the exercise below are: (i) put the main verbs in the sentence into the correct tense, and (ii) add words such as prepositions and articles so that the sentences make sense. Remember that the time expression in the sentence is a strong clue to the tense.

---

2 Telegramese

This question is always set in the form of a letter. The perfect tense is often used in letters because much of the content of a letter will be things that happened in the past but continue up to the point of writing or which have a strong present effect, i.e. news.

Make all the changes and additions necessary to produce, from the following sets of words and phrases, sentences which together make a complete letter. Write each sentence in the space provided.

4 Nash Road,
Burnley

14th January 1994

Dear Simon,

1 I be sorry / I not write sooner / I be so busy.

....

2 As you see / address above, / I move / new flat.

....

3 I unpack / since I arrive / I still not finish.

....

4 I move in / start of week / start / paint / Tuesday.

....

5 I not be / work / at all / past few days.

....

6 If fancy / break / you welcome / come / stay here.

....

7 I know / you always want / see this part of country.

....

8 They not connect / phone yet / write / if you plan / come.

....

Yours,

Bob

Unit 8 **Relative clauses**

> *Language focus:* defining and non-defining relative clauses; use of **whose, whom, where, when,** etc.; use of prepositions with relative clauses
>
> *Exam focus:*   cloze question

LEAD-IN

1 The extracts below are from *The Guinness Book of Records*, which contains information on all world records. Before reading them, discuss with another student what the records under the following headings might be about.

WORKING CAREER   BEARD OF BEES   STANDING   HUMAN COMPUTER

Now read the passages below to see if you were right.

1 *LONGEST ON A RAFT*

The longest recorded survival alone on a raft is 133 days by Second Steward Poon Lim of the UK Merchant Navy, *whose ship was torpedoed in the Atlantic in 1942.*

2 *WORKING CAREER*

The longest working life has been that of 98 years by Mr Izumi, *who began work herding animals at a sugar mill at Isen, Tokunashima, Japan in 1872.* He retired as a sugar cane farmer in 1970 aged 105.

3 *MOST TRAVELLED MAN*

The man *who had visited more countries than anyone* was Jesse Hart Rosdail (1914–77). Of all the separately administered countries and territories listed in the *UN Population Report*, he had visited all, excepting only North Korea and the French Antarctic Territories.

4 *BEARD OF BEES*

The ultimate beard of bees was achieved by Max Beck, 21, of Arcola, USA, *who, in 1985, managed to attract 70,000 bees, weighing 9kg, to his body.*

5 *STANDING*

The longest period on record *that anyone has continuously stood* is for more than seventeen years in the case of Swami Maujgiri Maharij when performing the *Tapasya* or penance from 1955 to November 1973 in Shahjahanpur, India. When sleeping he would lean against a plank. He died aged 85 in 1980.

6 *HUMAN COMPUTER*

Mrs Shakuntala Devi of India demonstrated the multiplication of two 13-digit numbers, 7,686,369,774,870 x 2,465,099,745,779, *which were picked at random by the Computer Department of Imperial College London in June 1980*, in 28 seconds.

(adapted from *The Guiness Book of Records 1987 and 1994*)

2 The grammatical term for the parts of the texts in italics is *relative clauses*. The two types of relative clause are described below.

    a Defining relative clauses tell us exactly which person or thing the writer is talking about. Removing a defining relative clause completely changes the meaning of a sentence.

       Example: *The man **who holds the record for golf-ball balancing** is Lang Martin. He balanced seven golf balls vertically without adhesive in 1980.*

    b Non-defining relative clauses give us extra information about the person or thing the writer is talking about. Removing a non-defining clause does not significantly change the meaning of a sentence.

       Example: *The oldest recorded bridegroom is Harry Stevens, 103, **who married 84-year-old Thelma Lucas at the Caravilla Retirement Home in Wisconsin.***

Look back at the extracts in Task 1 and decide whether the relative clauses they contain are (a) defining or (b) non-defining. Check your answers with another student.

3 Look at the extracts again and see if you can work out the rule for the use of commas with defining and non-defining relative clauses.

REFERENCE

1 In what type of relative clause are the following true? Read Sections A and B to find out and complete the chart with √s and Xs.

	Defining	*Non-defining*
Commas are used to separate the relative clause from the rest of the sentence		
The relative pronoun can be omitted		
That can be used instead of **who** or **which**		
When can be used as a relative pronoun		

A *Defining relative clauses*

  1 Defining relative clauses help us identify or define the thing we are talking about.

     A: *Do you know that man?*
     B: *What man?*
     A: *The man **who is talking to Mr Jones**.*

    We do not use commas before or after defining relative clauses.

  2 **Who** is typically used for people; **which** or **that** are used to talk about things. **That** is also used for people in informal speech.

    *Anyone **who** hasn't received a letter by now probably won't be called for interview. Even the train **that** left at 7 a.m. wouldn't have got us to London in time.*

3 **Who, that** and **which** are often left out when they are the object of a defining relative clause.

*I already know about the surprise **(which)** Peter has planned.* ('Peter' is the subject of the clause; 'which' is the object.)

But when **who, that** and **which** are the subject of a defining relative clause they cannot be left out.

*People **who** arrived late had to stand at the back.* (**not**: *People arrived late had to stand at the back.*)

4 Other relative pronouns in defining relative clauses are as follows:

*The woman **whose** house we're going to be staying in is quite a famous writer.* (possessive relative pronoun)
*Spring is the season **when** it's best to visit.* (used after nouns of time)
*There isn't a town in the southern half of the country **where** people can feel safe.* (used after nouns of place)
*I can't think of any reason **why** they should be late.* (used after the noun *reason*)

B Non-defining relative clauses

1 Non-defining relative clauses give extra information about a person or thing that we have already clearly identified in the sentence.
*The owner of the hotel, **who** had been at school with my mother, recognised her as soon as we walked in.*

A non-defining relative clause is separated from the rest of the sentence by commas.

2 In non-defining clauses **who** is used for people and **which** (not **that**) is used for things.
*I've received your letter, **which** I've passed on to my boss.*

3 We also use **which** in non-defining relative clauses when we want to talk about the whole previous clause.
*She's decided to go to college, **which** has really pleased her parents.*

4 In non-defining clauses we can never omit the relative pronoun.
   *The key is in my wallet, **which** I've left at home.*

5 Other relative pronouns and non-defining clauses are as follows:

*Margaret Spool, **whose** children's stories have won her international fame, has just produced her first novel.*
*Shall I call back later, **when** you're not quite so busy?* (used after expressions of time)
*I'll give you my friend's home number, **where** I can be reached most evenings.* (used after expressions of place)

2 Read the pairs of sentences below and match each sentence to one of the explanations (i) and (ii) that follow.

1 a) I chose the cat that still had its tail.
   b) I chose the cat, which still had its tail.

   i) I chose the cat, probably from a group of different animals. It still had its tail (perhaps some of the others didn't).
   ii) From a group of cats I chose the one with a tail.

2 a) I found the letter which she had been writing earlier in the sitting room.
   b) I found the letter, which she had been writing earlier, in the sitting room.

   i) She was writing the letter in the sitting room.
   ii) I found the letter in the sitting room.

3 a) He was wearing some sunglasses, which I liked.
   b) He was wearing some sunglasses that I liked.

   i) I liked the fact that he was wearing sunglasses.
   ii) I liked the sunglasses he was wearing.

4 a) To cheer her up I gave her a clock which worked.
   b) To cheer her up I gave her a clock, which worked.

   i) I gave her a clock and my action cheered her up.
   ii) I gave her a clock which worked, as opposed to one that didn't.

C *Prepositions with relative clauses*

1 In defining and non-defining relative clauses in conversation we usually place a dependent preposition at the end of the clause:

*The people (who) I was speaking **to** didn't seem interested.*
*I met Kevin, **who** I got the job **through**, quite by chance.*

In formal written English we often put the preposition before **whom** or **which**:

*That's the person **to whom** David was introduced.*

After a preposition we cannot use **who** and **that**; we can only use **whom** and **which**.

2 Note the special phrases in non-defining clauses:

some all both many much	of which	whom

*I made a lot of good friends at evening classes, **many of whom** I still see.*

3 Complete the sentences below with one of the relative clauses a–h and add any necessary punctuation. Then check your answers with another student.

1 It's important to find a house ....

2 The person .... is a good friend of mine.

3 My son's been to places ....

4 There is not going to be a strike ....

5 The director of the school .... used to work in Spain.

6 We're having a reunion of some old school friends ....

7 That old car over there ....
   is worth a lot of money.

8 I know a great resort ....

   a) that I've never heard of   e) you'll be meeting
   b) which has good amenities nearby   f) which is a great relief to everyone
   c) which I haven't used for years   g) where you have the beaches to yourself
   d) most of whom you'll recognise   h) whose name I forget

COMMUNICATIVE PRACTICE

1 The case of Samuel Ruddock

Read about the mysterious events that happened to Samuel Ruddock. Discuss with another student what seems strange about the story. The numbers and spaces in the text mark places where you could put the non-defining relative clauses a–k listed below. Solve the mystery and find the motive(s) for the crime by inserting the clauses in the text. The first one has been done for you.

Samuel Ruddock had been living alone in his large house since the departure of his children and wife (1) ...*a*... Samuel (2) .... went to bed on 6th November 1937 with his evening cup of tea (3) .... He made his way upstairs and, after checking that the windows were tightly secured, he locked the bedroom door and settled down into his large four-poster bed (4) .... The clock on the wall (5) .... had just chimed the first stroke of midnight as he fell into a deep sleep.

He awoke to the sound of three large policemen breaking down his bedroom door: they had been called after neighbours had heard a woman screaming. The clock (6) .... said it was one minute after midnight. Samuel found himself lying on the floor, next to the body of his estranged wife (7) .... She had been shot. The gun (8) .... was lying between them. The room (9) .... was completely empty except for the clock on the wall.

No one from the Police Department of Arkansas State (10) .... believed his story about going to bed at midnight. He was charged with the murder of his wife Jean (11) ....

a) which he had caused by his insensitivity to his wife's illness
b) which had been put forward an hour
c) from which everything (including the bed) had been removed
d) who had since written his children out of his will
e) which was just as she had planned
f) under which someone was hiding
g) which had now been put back an hour
h) which had a law making invalid any will written by someone insane
i) which he had at some time held
j) which had been drugged
k) whose doctor had predicted she had only three months to live

2 Collage connections

Look at the collage of pictures and images below and with another student try and identify two or three people or things between whom/which there is a connection.

Example: *Three symbols that represent different foreign currencies.*

Find as many connections as you can and write them down in the form of problems for other students to solve, using a relative clause.

Example: *Find three symbols that represent different foreign currencies.*

EXAM FOCUS

EXAM TIP 10

Punctuation

Looking at the punctuation of sentences can help you to work out the missing words. With relative clauses, for example, a comma before the blank which stands for a relative pronoun indicates a non-defining relative clause, so you would use **which**, not **that**, to talk about things.

In the following passages all the blanks are words which relate to the grammar of relative clauses covered in this unit.

1 Cloze

Fill each of the numbered blanks in the following passage. Use only *one* word in each space, or leave the space empty if no word is needed.

John Wyndham, (1) .... was born in 1903, lived in Edgbaston, Birmingham, until 1911 and then in many other parts of England. After attending several English preparatory schools he went to Bedales School from 1918 till 1921. Careers (2) .... he tried included farming, law, commercial art and advertising, and he first started writing short stories (3) .... were intended for sale, in 1925. From 1930 till 1939 he wrote stories of different kinds for American publications but the names under (4) .... he wrote varied. During the war he was in the Civil Service and afterwards in the Army. In 1946 he went back to writing short stories, (5) .... which he had some success in the USA, and he decided to try a modified form of what is unhappily known as 'science fiction'. He wrote *The Day of the Triffids* and *The Kraken Wakes*, ((6) .... of which have been translated into several languages), *The Chrysalids* and *The Midwich Cuckoos*, (7) .... was made into a film entitled *The Village of the Damned*. He wrote many other fine novels, (8) .... titles include *The Seeds of Time*, *Trouble with Lichen* and *The Outward Urge*, all (9) .... which have been published by Penguin Books. John Wyndham died in March 1969, at a time (10) .... man was about to take his first steps on the moon.

(adapted from the Introduction to *The Day of the Triffids*, Penguin 1987)

Unit 9 Verb and object patterns

> *Language focus:* transitive and intransitive verbs; verbs with direct and indirect objects; use of **to** and **for** with indirect objects
>
> *Exam focus:* multiple-choice and telegramese questions

LEAD-IN

Not all verbs in English can be used with objects. For example, you can't 'disappear something' – you have to say 'something disappears'.

Verbs that *can* be used with objects (e.g. **hit** something) do not all follow the same object pattern. For example:

The car hit a tree. (verb + direct object)
He gave me a book. (verb + indirect and direct objects)

1 Working with another student, fit the jigsaw pieces below into the jigsaw board. For a piece to fit it must be both the right shape and fit grammatically with the verb. One line has been done for you.

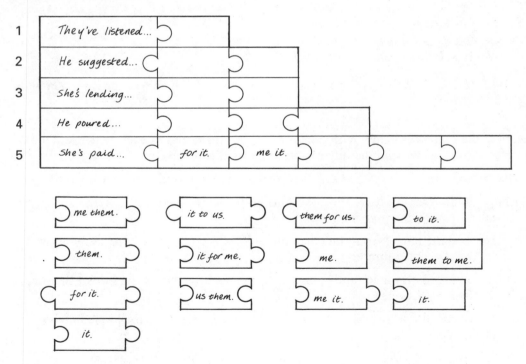

2 Look back at line 5 in the puzzle. Working with another student, try and work out what kind of noun *it* could stand for in each case.

REFERENCE

A Transitive and intransitive verbs

1 *Transitive* verbs are those which are followed by an object:
*Someone in the crowd **threw a stone** which **hit the policeman.***

They can be used in the passive form:
*The pupils **were welcomed** by the school principal.*

2 *Intransitive* verbs are those which cannot be used with an object:
*My passport **has disappeared.***
*No one **has arrived** yet.*

Verbs which are typically used intransitively are:

appear	arrive	consist	decline	depart	die	disappear	drip
fall	flow	grow	happen	itch	lie	listen	recur	rise
succeed (meaning 'have success')		vibrate	wait				

We can thus *not* say: *he succeeded the test*, or *the rain grew the flowers* or *they listened the children to the music.*

To express such meanings we need to use an alternative transitive verb – *He **passed** the test* – or a structure with **make** or **let**:
*The rain **made** the flowers grow.*
*They **let** the children listen to the music.*

NOTE: Intransitive verbs cannot be used in the passive form. We cannot say: *The plan was succeeded.*

---

1 Complete the sentences below with one of the verbs at the end of each sentence. One of the verbs is intransitive and the other is typically used transitively.

1 Unemployment .... to record levels last month.   (raise / rise)

2 Many children had to leave the cities during the war and were .... by strangers.   (bring up / grow up)

3 He grabbed the parcel from the postman and .... it to see what was inside.   (shake / vibrate)

4 The car skidded on the ice and .... a litter bin at the side of the road. (knock over / fell over)

5 If signs of the illness .... , contact your local doctor immediately. (recur / repeat)

6 You'll never .... your ambitions if you don't work harder (achieve / succeed)

7 Several guests have .... the hotel this morning and taken their keys with them.   (depart / leave)

8 Has anyone .... anything to you about getting our money back for the trip we missed?   (say / speak)

9 The number of students enrolling in courses at the language school is .... (reduce / decline)

10 I accidentally knocked my cup over and .... coffee on the new carpet. (spill / drip)

B *Transitive verbs and object patterns*

1 Many common verbs have two objects: a direct object and an indirect object.
*The waiter **showed** me the menu.*

(**me** is the indirect object, **the menu** is the direct object)

2 The indirect object can also be introduced by the prepositions **to** or **for**. In this case, it comes *after* the direct object:
*She didn't want to tell the bad news **to the children**.*

(compare: *She didn't want to tell the children the bad news.*)

The preposition is usually used when the indirect object is a longer phrase.
*My mother **has lent** our spare television **to the elderly man next door**.*
*The child **saved** a seat **for the friend she was expecting**.*

Verbs typically used in this way with **to** are:

give	lend	pass	promise	read
rent	send	show	tell	write

Verbs typically used in this way with **for** are:

book	buy	draw	leave	make	pour
prepare	reserve	save	steal	take	

3 Verb + direct object + **to** + indirect object
There is a certain group of verbs in English with which we *have to* use **to** before an indirect object.
*He **explained** the scheme **to the foreign visitors**.*
We cannot say: *He explained the foreign visitors the scheme.*

Verbs which follow this pattern are:

address	admit	describe	explain	introduce
mention	propose	recommend	suggest	

2 Complete the sentences below with the two 'objects' given in brackets at the end of each sentence. Think about in which *order* they should be used and whether you need to *add a preposition or not.*

Example: *The man in the market **sold** me a broken watch.*   (a broken watch / me)

1 That's the estate agent that got ....
(the house / my parents)

2 She hasn't managed to **prove** ....
(anyone / her innocence)

3 When was the last time the headmaster **ordered** .... ?
(the school / any new equipment)

4 The happy father rushed out to **announce** ....
(the rest of the family / the news)

5 The college **has offered** ....
(my sister / a place on the course)

6 The company **owes** ....
(a foreign bank / a large sum of money)

7 Some people I knew from work **found** ....
(the flat / us)

8 I'd like you to **teach** ....
(French / all the classes in the school)

Find the two verbs in this exercise which follow the pattern of the verbs in Section B (3).

COMMUNICATIVE PRACTICE

1 Fairytales

First tell another student what you know about these fairytales.

a) Cinderella   b) Little Red Riding Hood   c) The Three Bears
d) Snow White and the Seven Dwarfs   e) Jack and the Beanstalk

Now, working with another student, complete sentences 1–8 on the opposite page to make a true statement about an event in one of the fairytales. To do this use two of the words (direct / indirect objects) from the box below. You may need to add a preposition. Then put in the brackets at the end of each sentence a letter to show which fairytale you are talking about.

Example: *A woman gave her son a cow. (e)*

her son	their sister	one of her hosts	dinner	his mother
some food	her	her grandmother	herself	a golden hen
someone else's name	a shoe	nothing to eat	a prince	seven men
her grandmother's hands	her	a cow		

1 A little girl decided to go through the forest to take   (.....)

2 Two women laughed when someone offered   (.....)

3 A queen got angry when her mirror suggested   (.....)

4 A poor boy stole   (.....)

5 A little girl with golden hair left   (.....)

6 A girl didn't introduce   (.....)

7 A lovely woman regularly prepared   (.....)

8 A loving child described   (.....)

2 Noughts and crosses

The game on the board below is played in a similar way to a normal game of noughts and crosses. One player is 'noughts' and the other 'crosses'. The object of the game is to get a row of three XXX or three OOO.

Play with another student. Using one of the grids on the board, choose a square and make an offer to your partner about the picture or words in the square, using one of the verbs on the board. You must use the words *you / your / to you / for you*. No verb can be used twice in any one game.

Example: *Grid 1: I can recommend a hotel to you.*

If your partner thinks that your offer makes sense, and is grammatically correct, you can put your nought or cross on the square. If not, he / she must explain why. If you can't agree, ask your teacher to act as judge.

EXAM FOCUS

1 Multiple-choice

Before answering each question, write which grammar label from the box below describes the grammar point being tested in each sentence. Then choose the word or phrase which best completes the sentence by circling the letter A, B, C or D.

> verb + indirect object   transitive verb pattern
> verb with two objects   intransitive verb pattern
> verb + preposition + indirect object

1 One of the guides .... me how the machine worked.

    A proposed   B explained   C said   D showed   ....

2 Our sales figures have been slowly .... all year.

    A reducing   B raising   C declining   D losing   ....

3 The child eventually .... the judge the truth.

    A said   B told   C mentioned   D spoke   ....

4 I opened the letter even though it was not addressed ....

    A me   B to me   C for me   D it me   ....

5 The astronauts were pleased with the results of the mission even though all its aims were not ....

    A achieved   B managed   C succeeded   D arrived   ....

6 The owner of the restaurant said that he could not .... a place for us.

    A give   B offer   C wait   D reserve   ....

7 The guests at the party .... drink everywhere.

    A dripped   B flowed   C spilt   D fell   ....

8 I knew how to drive because my mother had taught .... when we lived abroad.

    A it me   B to me   C me   D me for it   ....

9 They had no idea how to replace the money which had been .... as a result of the robbery.

    A disappeared   B lost   C departed   D gone   ....

10 New accommodation was .... for me when the local council knocked down my old block of flats.

    A found   B offered   C promised   D owed   ....

EXAM TIP 10

What and what not to put in

Unlike the cloze question, the telegramese
question can tempt you to put in a word where
none is needed. With verbs and the objects that
follow them, you will have to make decisions
about: (i) what kind of object pattern the verb
takes, and (ii) whether you need to use a
preposition before the object.

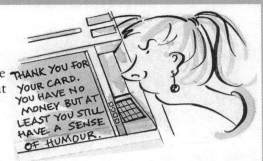

THANK YOU FOR YOUR CARD. YOU HAVE NO MONEY BUT AT LEAST YOU STILL HAVE A SENSE OF HUMOUR.

2 Telegramese

Make all the changes and additions necessary to produce, from the following sets of
words and phrases, sentences which together make a complete letter. Write each sentence
in the space provided.

> 14 Arch Street,
> Wimbledon,
> London
>
> 17th May 1994

Dear Pete,

1 Thank you / offer me / chance / stay you / Spain / this summer.

....

2 I discuss it / my parents / they say / I can come.

....

3 They insist / I pay / accommodation / myself though.

....

4 I mention Jenny / I go / she lend me / Spanish music / I listen now.

....

5 I hardly wait / summer / arrive.

....

6 I promise Jenny / I show her photo / place we go.

....

7 Please send / if have one.

....

8 I address this / old address / I hope / get it / before you move / new flat.

....

> Yours,
>
> Elizabeth

Unit 10 Comparatives and superlatives

Language focus: comparative and superlative forms of adjectives and adverbs; (not) as . . . as; words and expressions that can be used before comparatives

Exam focus: transformation and cloze questions

LEAD-IN

1 Read through the text and decide whether the highlighted words are (a) comparative adjective forms, or (b) comparative adverb forms. Check your answers with another student.

Improve your memory

Did you know that everything you have ever read or seen is stored somewhere in your memory? The problem is that you can't always get at it. And when you can't get at something in your memory, you say you have a poor memory. In fact, you don't have a poor memory at all – you have a wonderful memory. But to use that memory (1) **more effectively** it has to be trained.

That's why memory training is such an important part of the unique Pelman Home Study Course. As a Pelman student, your personal tutor will guide you through a series of lessons which become progressively (2) **more difficult** – each one based on programmed learning techniques that will train your memory to achieve a (3) **higher** level of performance.

INSTANT RECALL

This is possible because your memory is like a muscle. Without exercise it gets flabby. But with the right kind of training, you'll be able to recall things much (4) **faster**.

Right from the start you will feel your memory muscles getting (5) **stronger** – your powers of recall ever (6) **quicker**.

Many people just do not realise how much they can improve their memories and the extent to which it can make them (7) **more successful** in their business and social lives. There is simply no one who cannot learn to retain things (8) **longer** and recall things (9) **more quickly**. A trained memory can truly be a passport to a (10) **better** life!

WHO CAN BENEFIT?
- Students
- Salespeople
- Managers
- Office workers
- Industrial workers
- Professional people
- In fact, anyone!

The human brain

(adapted from a Pelman advertisement)

2 Below are two incomplete grammar rules about: (a) how to form comparative adjectives, and (b) how to form comparative adverbs.

By looking at the evidence from the Improve your memory advertisement, complete each rule using the language in the box below. Work with another student to do this.

add -er	more	e.g. **quickly**	more	longer	one syllable
e.g. **fast runner/run fast**	-er ending				

a To form the comparative form of adjectives with (1) ....

e.g. **quick**, (2) .... With words of more than one

syllable, e.g. **successful**, use (3) .... in front of the word.

b To form the comparative form of adverbs use (1) ....

in front of those adverbs which have an **-ly** ending (2) ....

Adjectives, however, which have the same adverb form (3) ....

.... also have the same (4) ....

in the adverb form, e.g. (5) ....

REFERENCE

1 Use this exercise to see how much you already know about the comparative forms of adjectives and adverbs. Complete each sentence below with one of the words or phrases which follow it. Discuss your answers with another student and then check your answers by looking at Sections A–E below.

1   The USA is probably the world's .... country.   (richer / richest)

2   Can we go somewhere .... to talk?   (quieter / more quiet)

3   I can't remember a spring that was .... than this.   (hoter / hotter)

4   I really think she talks even .... than she used to.
    (quicker / more quickly)

5   The meal was all right, but it was .... the film.
    (less good than / not as good as)

6   The costumes and lighting were terrible and the acting was .... as bad.
    (even / just)

7   Of all the countries I've been to, France is the one of which I have .... the
    fondest memories.   (by far / far)

8   Chinese is the most widely spoken language .... the world.   (in / of)

A Adjectives: Comparative and superlative forms

Adjective	Comparative form	Superlative form
Adjectives of one syllable: high fast warm cheap	**-er** higher faster warmer richer	**the -est** the highest the fastest
Adjectives of more than one syllable: expensive difficult helpful	**more . . . less** more expensive more difficult less helpful	**the most . . . the least** the most expensive the most difficult the least helpful
Irregular forms: good bad far	good – better bad – worse far – further	good – the best bad – the worst far – the furthest

Life just seems to be getting **more expensive** each week.
Taking the train proved to be **the cheapest** option.
Christmas is one of **the warmest** times of the year in Australia.

NOTE: Some comparative forms involve a change of spelling:
big – bigger   hot – hotter   fat – fatter   happy – happier   easy – easier

And a few two-syllable words also have the **-er/-est** comparative/superlative form:
quieter, narrower, simpler.

B Adverbs: Comparative and superlative forms

Adverb	Comparative form	Superlative form
Adverbs with -ly ending carefully clearly	**more** carefully **less** clearly	**the most** carefully **the least** clearly
Adverbs with same *form as adjective:* fast hard high	**-er** faster harder	**the -est** the fastest the hardest

Do your homework **more carefully** and you'll get better marks.
I work **harder** than anyone but no one seems to notice.
I was surprised that of all the speakers the Prime Minister spoke **the least clearly**.

C as . . . as

When comparing things we can also use adjectives and adverbs with (**not**) **as . . . as**.
The car looks **as new as** *when we bought it.*
Your son is behaving just **as aggressively as** *before.*
That clock isn't **as reliable as** *the one in the kitchen.*

Not as . . . (as) is used instead of **less** with one-syllable adjectives / adverbs that usually have an **-er** comparative form.

*My father hasn't been working **as hard as** he used to. (not: less hard.)*
*The exam wasn't **as easy as** the last one. (not: less easy than.)*

D Words and expressions used before comparatives

even	a lot	much	far	a bit	any	. . . (lazier / more helpful)

just	every bit	not nearly	nowhere near	. . . (as lazy as)

*This car is **even slower** than the last one we had.*
*Have we got **much further** to go?*
*The team were **nowhere near as good** in defence this year.*
*The countryside must suit you: you seem **a lot more relaxed**.*

The phrase **by far** can also be used with superlatives in a similar way.

*Come on, don't be modest. I've heard you were **by far the best** student **in the class**.*

Also note this use of the preposition **in** after superlatives.

2 Work with another student and match the half sentences on the left to those on the right to form complete sentences.

1	The journey by train was less	a)	easier this time round.
2	The seats on trains are nowhere near as	b)	more smoothly this time.
3	We can deliver parcels even more	c)	further than I thought.
4	I found the exam	d)	enjoyable than before.
5	With the right tool we finished it	e)	well as it could have.
6	The team did not perform as	f)	nice these days.
7	We must have walked	g)	much more easily.
8	Of all the performances, his was the	h)	most hospitable of all.
9	The whole event went far	i)	least convincing.
10	The people we met there were the	j)	quickly than before.

COMMUNICATIVE PRACTICE

1 Superlative impostor

Look at the lists of four things / people / places below. In each list, there are three true superlatives; that is, the biggest, highest, most valuable, etc. One thing in each list is an impostor: that is, it may only be the second or third biggest, best, etc. With two or three other students, look at each list and discuss which one the impostor might be.

1 SIZE: Lake Michigan   the Pacific Ocean   the River Nile   the Caspian Sea

2 AREA: Canada   Asia   Russia   Greenland

3 MONEY: USA   the Sultan of Brunei   Van Gogh   gold

4 NUMBER OF PEOPLE: Mexico City   China   English   Chinese

5 SIZE: Mount Everest   the Empire State Building   Jupiter   the Sahara

6 WEATHER CONDITIONS: Ethiopia   Antarctica   the North Pole   Bangladesh

7 ANIMALS: leopard   ostrich   great white shark   giraffe

2 Where on earth am I?

Look at the map of the world and identify a country that you know reasonably well and can answer simple questions on, such as on climate and population.

The other members of the class have to find out which country you have chosen. They can ask you ten questions, all of which have to be in the form of comparatives.

Example questions:

Is the country further north than (Egypt)?
Does the country have a warmer climate than (Britain)?
Does it have borders with more than one other country?
Is it as industrialised as (Western European countries)?
Is the capital of the country larger than (Paris)?
Which is closer to the country: (Japan) or (Norway)?

Example answers:

Yes, much . . . -er.   No, not at all.
Yes, a bit more.   No, nowhere near.
Yes, quite a lot more.   No, not as . . . as.
                               No, much less . . . .

Before you start, prepare a few questions which you might ask to identify the general part of the world a country is in and two or three questions which might help you to identify a country more specifically.

EXAM FOCUS

EXAM TIP 12

Putting it another way

Expressing something in a different way not only means finding a substitute phrase but it often means making grammatical changes to the sentence. You must carefully check that you have made all the changes necessary when writing your substitute phrase into the new sentence.

1 Transformation

Finish each of the following sentences in such a way that it means the same as the sentence printed before it. Use the phrases in the box to replace the phrases in bold print in the sentences.

> as well as   much faster   the cheapest   as cheaply as
> a lot further   not as cheap as   just as many   not nearly as
> more than any other   even worse

1 I didn't realise we had wandered **such a long way** from the path.

   We had ....

2 My friend has always been able to cook **better than** me.

   I have ....

3 Going by car **takes a lot longer** than going by train.

   Going by train ....

4 I'm afraid I don't have **a cheaper one** in stock.

   I'm afraid this ....

5 Michael Jackson is the performer I would **most** like to see live in concert.

   I'd like ....

6 We had to **pay more** for the tickets than I expected.

   The tickets ....

7 We had **the same number** of players injured as the other team.

   The other team ....

8 The test was **much easier** than I thought it would be.

   The test was ....

9 I hated the resort and liked the hotel **even less.**

   I thought the hotel ....

10 They were asking **higher prices** than usual for front row tickets.

   They weren't selling ....

2 Cloze

The following passage is about the USA's vast open state of Wyoming and the important part this state has played in the shaping of American history.

Fill each of the numbered blanks in the passage. Use only *one* word in each space.

Wyoming is the USA's (1) .... populated state. No other state has (2) ....

people – only 465,000. There are no big cities. The (3) .... city of the few that

there are is the capital Cheyenne, home to 50,000 people. Yet the state is rich in mineral

deposits, natural beauty and history. Coal lies under 55 per cent of Wyoming and in the

Powder River Basin towering coal silos announce from a distance that you are approaching

the largest coal mine (4) .... the Americas, Black Thunder. Indeed, it was here in

the wilderness that I saw (5) .... far the biggest dump truck that I had

(6) .... seen.

   Historically, South Pass – the old Oregon wagon trail – is Wyoming's (7) ....

significant landmark. South Pass offered the (8) .... , though not the most direct,

wagon route for settlers over the Rocky Mountains, and had it not been for South Pass, the

USA might be (9) .... smaller today. South Pass City, born in a gold boom, played

another key role in US history. Its governing body, the Wyoming Territorial Legislature, proved

itself to be (10) .... most progressive in the world when it became the first

governing body to extend full voting rights to women.

(adapted from Thomas J. Abercrombie 'Wide Open Wyoming', National Geographic)

Unit 11 The future

LEAD-IN

1 Complete your 'futurescope' below with information about yourself. Make notes in each of the boxes.

Collect photos this afternoon.

Your Arrangements for later today

The next earthquake in Slovakia
A resolution for the rest of the year

Your Holiday plans

Your level of English in the year 2000: a prediction
You and FCE: a prediction

Career / job in ten years' time

2 Now look at this short text about a famous British actor and match the highlighted verb phrases to the future meanings a–e.

a) talking about intentions
b) talking about arrangements
c) making predictions

d) talking about a future action in progress at a particular time
e) talking about timetables / schedules

Blessed to attempt an Everest record

Actor Brian Blessed aims to push back the frontier of middle age by being the oldest man to climb Mount Everest.

"It's not how old you are, it's how you're old," said Blessed, who climbed to 26,000 feet in his first attempt on Everest three years ago.

His obsession with Everest goes back to his childhood hero George Mallory, who disappeared near the summit in 1924. It was Mallory who, when asked why he wanted to climb Everest, gave the celebrated reply: "Because it is there."

Blessed said: (1) "We **'ll** probably never **know** if Mallory made it to the summit, and I wholly embrace the mystery."

The attempt (2) **begins** next Tuesday

"IT'S NOT HOW OLD YOU ARE, IT'S HOW YOU'RE OLD."

when the group set off for base camp . As part of his mission Blessed (3) **is going to place** on top of Everest a white scarf given to him by the Dalai Lama. "He's asked me to recite a mantra and a peace prayer for the world."

Blessed (4) **is** also **taking** with him a teddy bear which is to be auctioned later to raise money for children suffering from cancer.

Blessed says he wants to spend the rest of his life devoting six months a year to acting and the other six to adventure. This time next year (5) **he'll be setting off** in search of the Abominable Snowman. "I want to climb the highest summit on each of the seven continents, plug the ozone hole, explore the bottom of the sea," he said.

(adapted from the *Evening Standard*)

3 Look back at your 'futurescope' and make your notes into full sentences. Think carefully about the verb form in each case.

Example: *I'm collecting my photos this afternoon.*

Now ask your partner questions to find out about the information in his / her futurescope. Think carefully about the verb form you use in your questions.

Example:

A: *What are you doing later today?*
B: *I'm going home for dinner first, then meeting some friends.*

REFERENCE

Main forms used to express future meaning

1 Will

Affirmative	*Negative*
I will (I'll, etc.) come, etc.	I will not (won't) come, etc.

Question	*Short answers*
Will you come?	Yes, I will. No, I won't.

2 Be going to

Affirmative	*Negative*
I am (I'm) going to come, etc.	I am not (I'm not) going to come, etc.

Question	*Short answers*
Are you going to come?	Yes, I am. No, I'm not.

3 Present continuous

I am coming, etc.

Uses

1 Will

a Will is used to make predictions based on a personal opinion or what the speaker believes to be the usual course of events.

We'll have time for a drink before the film starts.
The train won't get us there in time.

It is often used with this kind of meaning with the following verbs and phrases:

I think, I expect, I doubt, I suppose, I guess, I'm sure.

I doubt there will be anything to eat, just drinks.
The police will search fans as they enter the stadium, I suppose.

b The contracted form of **will** (**'ll**) is used when the speaker decides something at the moment of speaking.

'Please come, Ruth, everyone's expecting you.'
'OK, stop going on, I'll come.'

c **Will** is also used with the following kinds of meaning.

Requests and offers:

Will you help me do the garden later?
Don't worry, I'll help you with whatever needs doing.

Promises and threats:

I promise I'll be there on time.
We won't let you have your friends round if you don't tidy your room.

Refusals:

Our shop won't give you your money back without the receipt.
The matches won't light, they're too damp.

Also: machines and illnesses:

The fridge door won't shut.
My cold won't go away.

NOTE: **Shall** is not typically used instead of **will** in everyday English but is used in the interrogative form with **I** and **we** to ask for and make suggestions and to make offers.

Shall we go to the Italian restaurant for a change?
What shall I do if he's not in?
I'll make you a cup of tea, shall I?

d In sentences involving link words and phrases such as **when, before, after, as soon as, in case** and **until** we usually only use **will** *once* in the sentence.

I'll give you a ring as soon as I've heard from her.
I'll give you the phone number in case you get lost.

1 Complete the sentences with one word in each gap. Use contracted forms if you want to.

1 I really .... expect that they .... turn up this late.

2 .... I call back later if you're busy?

3 You'll probably be too tired to come, I .... ?

4 I'm phoning to tell you I .... be late. The car .... start.

5 We're stuck here until Philip arrives, so what .... we do while we're waiting?

6 I .... phone Sarah in case she .... know we're coming.

7 I .... return the book to you as soon as I .... read it.

8 I .... if she .... recognise you. You've really changed.

2 Be going to

a **Be going to** is used when someone has a definite intention or plan to do something. It can express determination to do something.

*The council **is going to** knock down the old cinema to make a new shopping centre.*
*I**'m going to** go tonight whether you like it or not.*

b **Be going to** is used to make or ask for predictions in response to something which exists in the present situation.

*Look, that child **is going to** fall if she's not careful!*
*Who **is going to** clean up this mess?*

3 Present continuous

The present continuous tense is used to talk about definite arrangements / fixed plans in the future, such as ones that appear in appointment books and calendar programmes.
*We**'re not having** the barbeque on Sunday now, I'm afraid.*
*The BBC **are showing** Sunday's match live in twenty-six countries.*

It is used with a definite future time reference, whether stated (as a time phrase) or understood.

2 **Complete the sentences by putting the verb at the end of each sentence into the correct form to express future meaning.**

1 I'll have to prepare the meal before we .... out. (go)

2 I've got a terrible headache which .... away. (not / go)

3 .... we .... at your place, say about sixish? (meet)

4 I can't meet you on Friday, the plumber .... (come)

5 OK, you've convinced me, we .... the train. (take)

6 I .... this essay even if I have to stay up all night. (finish)

7 .... anyone .... that phone?
(not / answer)

8 Do you know how you .... to the party yet? (get)

9 We .... the children while you go shopping. (look after)

10 The town .... the annual spring festival on 5th May this year. (hold)

4 Present simple

The present simple is used with future meaning when talking about timetables or programmes of events.
*The 100m race **starts** at two o'clock after the long-jump final.*
*The train **arrives** at platform four and **departs** at 4.15.*

> NOTE: We use the present form of **to be** in the following phrases with future meaning:
> *I would invite you in but **we're about to** go out.*
> *Today's news means thousands **are likely to** lose their jobs.*
> *Jack's **supposed to** come too but I don't think he will.*
> *Don't worry about the exam, you're **bound to** pass.*

3 Match these examples to the different uses described in Boxes 5–6 below. Write the examples in the boxes.

1 I'll be calling in later, can I bring you anything?
2 By the time I retire I'll have worked here for twenty-three years.
3 We will have built the new stadium by next season.
4 I'm sure the restaurant will be making money before long.
5 I've got a letter for Henry. Will you be seeing him today?
6 I won't have finished the report before the meeting.
7 This time next week I'll be lying in the sun in Greece.
8 We'll have been married six years this April.

---

5 Future continuous

> I / you / he / she / it / we / they **will + be +** verb **+ ing**
>
> **a** The future continuous tense is used to predict an action that will be in progress at some time in the future. Examples:
>
> ....
>
> ....
>
> **b** It is sometimes used when talking or asking about personal plans. This form sounds slightly more formal than the present continuous. Examples:
>
> ....
>
> ....

6 Future perfect

> I / you / he / she / it / we / they **will + have +** past participle
>
> **a** The future perfect tense is used to talk about an action or event which will, or will not, be complete at some specific point in the future. Examples:
>
> ....
>
> ....
>
> **b** It is used to talk about the length of time an action will have lasted at some point in the future. Examples:
>
> ....
>
> ....

4 Recording the use of a particular time phrase with a particular tense is a useful way of remembering how a tense is used. Look at the unfinished sentences and the future time phrases below. Write in the boxes phrases that could complete each sentence. Some words can be used with both sentences.

as you read this letter   until tomorrow   on time   by March
all day tomorrow   before then   for a few weeks   soon

1 I'll be working there . . .

2 I'll have finished it . . .

COMMUNICATIVE PRACTICE

1 That's not it

Get into groups of two or three and then write four or five cards as follows:

Think of a famous person (politician, sports person, film star, etc.) or someone in your school who is known to the rest of the class.

Take a strip of paper or card and on one side write his or her name *in large letters*. On the other side, write some true information about this person's *future*. It might be :

future arrangement   *future plan*   or   *future happening*

is visiting China   *is going to announce*   *will be celebrating*

but *not a prediction*.

How to play

1 In turns, each group holds up a card so that the rest of the class can see the name.

2 The rest of the class then have to find out the information on the back of the card by asking questions like:

Isn't he going to produce a new album with . . . ?

The group with the card answers 'Yes' or 'No'.

3 The group who ask the correct question are given the card. The group with the most cards at end of the game are the winners.

2 Stock exchange

Working with another student, imagine that you have £1,000 to invest in three of the stocks below. Which stocks are likely to go up or down in value? Read the newspaper headlines and think about how the news stories may affect the value of the stocks. (The prices given are the real prices of the stocks on the London Stock Exchange on 7th December 1993, and the headlines are from newspapers of the same day.)

When you have made your decisions, your teacher will tell you how each stock finished that day and you can work out how much you have gained or lost.

Company	Opening price	Your investment	Closing share price: up or down
ERA Toys	0.10		
Midlands Electricity	6.53		
Iceland Foods*	1.54		
British Petroleum	3.26		
British Airways	4.33		
Manchester United†	5.37		

*a chain of food shops
†a football team

Worst winter in years still to come

More Britons seeking Xmas in the sun

Weather keeps seasonal shoppers at home

Further fall in oil price

BP chief says cost-cutting plan is working

Iceland Foods still opposed to Sunday trading

MANCHESTER UNITED WIN AGAIN

EXAM FOCUS

> ### EXAM TIP 13
>
> ### Your words in my reply
>
> It is very common in dialogue for someone to use some, or even all, of the words from the previous speaker's turn. Be aware of this in the dialogue building question, where you have to write questions or responses which fit exactly with what is said before and after. Read the whole dialogue carefully and make sure you understand the line(s) after each gap.

1 Dialogue building

Complete the numbered gaps in the following conversation. Stella is phoning her friend Kim to invite her to a party.

Stella: Hi, Kim, it's Stella here. How are you?

Kim: Fine, what about you?

Stella: Not bad, thanks. I'm ringing to invite you and Bill round on Wednesday. We're having a party for Jim's birthday.

Kim: I didn't know it was his birthday. (1) .... ?

Stella: Thirty. That's why I've decided to throw a party.

Kim: (2) .... ?

Stella: Oh, you know, the usual crowd, plus some of Jim's friends from work.

Kim: (3) .... ?

Stella: No, not quite as wild as the last one. I don't want to have to deal with the neighbours again. Anyway, can you come?

Kim: Of course, I wouldn't miss it for the world. I (4) .... and help you with the food.

Stella: OK, come early but I don't want you to help with the food. I want you to keep Jim out of the way.

Kim: What do you mean?

Stella: (5) ....

Kim: A surprise!

Stella: Yes, he thinks we (6) ....

Kim: I see, so Bill and I are the friends he's supposed to go to the pub with. But (7) ....

.... ?

Stella: Oh that's easy, I'll just say I'm staying in to cook you a meal. By the time you get back

           everyone (8) ....

Kim: . . . and have started without us, I bet.

2 Telegramese

Make all the changes and additions necessary to produce, from the following sets of
words and phrases, sentences which together make a complete letter. Write each sentence
in the space provided.

UK Study Tours,
2 Park Rd,
Norwich

31st July 1994

Dear Mme Esteve,

1 I write / inform you / final arrangements / your trip / next month.

....

2 Your group / stay / Campton Hall / most beautiful building / the University.

....

3 As agreed / your group / have English lessons / together / group Spanish students.

....

4 Group from Spain / arrive / Tuesday after you / lessons not begin / until Wednesday.

....

5 I be sure / you be happy / use / extra free days / sightseeing.

....

6 Norwich Festival / be about / begin / this week / many events / still go on / when arrive.

....

7 Students / also be able / use / sports facilities / Campton Hall / all day.

....

8 We look forward / see you / next month.

....

With kind regards,
Yours sincerely,

Trevor Ashcroft

Unit 12 **Prepositions**

Language focus: prepositions of place, movement and time; other prepositional phrases
Exam focus: cloze and telegramese questions

LEAD-IN

In Unit 6 we looked at dependent prepositions where adjectives like *rude,* and verbs like *depend* were seen to be followed by certain prepositions: *rude to* and *depend on.*

Prepositions are also common in structures called prepositional phrases. These are phrases where a preposition is used with another word, most commonly a noun. In these phrases the use of the preposition is related more to the word following the preposition rather than the word preceding it.

*I'd seen the man **at the window** before.*
*They got **in the car** and left.*

Working with another student, look at the ways Students A and B have recorded prepositional phrases. Then put the following prepositions in the room as Student A would do, and the prepositional phrases you are thinking of on the cards like Student B.

on   in   at   by   out of

Student A

Student B

REFERENCE

Sections A–D below cover the most commonly confused prepositions of place, movement and time.

A *Place:* in, at, on

1 **In** is mainly used with the meaning of 'inside something'.
*The knife is **in** the box **in** the kitchen drawer.*

In is also used when talking about places as areas: towns, cities, countries, etc.
*We live **in** Augsburg, which is **in** southern Germany.*

2 **At** is used to talk about the location of something when the location is understood as a point rather than a surface or enclosed space.
*I saw her face **at** the window.*

At is also used when talking about public places or institutions: shops, public facilities, addresses, etc.
*Several demonstrators are being held **at** the police station.*

At is also used when talking about places as stopping points on a journey somewhere.
*This train doesn't stop **at** either Winchurch or Barnhurst.*

3 **On** is used mainly when talking about surfaces: walls, tables, floors, etc.
*Don't hang the picture **on** the wall until I've dusted it.*

On is also used when talking about a place we think of as being in the shape of a line, e.g. a road, a river, a coast.
*What's the speed limit **on** a British motorway?*

NOTE: After verbs of movement when the idea is 'going from one place to another' we usually use the preposition **to**.
*The last time I went **to** Hong Kong was in 1984. (not: in Hong Kong)*

1 Working with another student, discuss where you would find the following signs and labels. Write your answer under each picture.

Example: WIPE YOUR FEET *on a doormat*

WIPE YOUR FEET

1

VISITING FANS ONLY

2

BABY ON BOARD

3

Don't feed the animals

4

6 SIDE A

7 SIZE 45

COMING SOON

5

8

Do not disturb

1 ....

2 ....

3 ....

4 ....

5 ....

6 ....

7 ....

8 ....

B *Movement:* off, into, onto, out of, over, under, down from, towards, away from, round

Complete your own reference section for these prepositions by matching them to the pictures in Exercise 2.

2 Working with another student, decide which preposition you would need to use to describe the movements of the cat in the picture below.

Example: *Picture 1 – into.*

C *Time:* in, at, on

3 Complete the table below by writing down one or two examples for each category and writing in the correct preposition in each box. Look at the examples already done for you.

Times	.... five o'clock / ....
Parts of the day	....
Days	.... weekdays ....
Dates	....
Weekends and public holidays	....
Months	....
Seasons	....
Years	.... the sixties, 1945 ....
Centuries	....

EXCEPTIONS: **Which preposition would you use with:**

1 .... night?   2 .... Thursday evening?

D *Other prepositional phrases*

There are many other prepositional phrases in English which do not follow any particular pattern. As a learner, you need to spot a particular phrase and then work out how it is used.

4 Look at the chart below. Complete each box with the preposition that can be used with all the words in the box.

.... cash danger the dark public	.... duty the phone the stairs the way
.... home the foot of the moment work	.... chance cheque myself post
.... a ride a walk now the time being	.... breath control danger order

Now put the words below into the correct box in the chart above.

least	the past	holiday	mistake	bounds	silence	a joke	luck
accident	ages	date	a bad mood	strike	once	last	heart
my own	shorts	sight	purpose	respect	a diet	a change	war

5 Complete the sentences with phrases from the box you have just completed above.

1 We stumbled about for a few minutes .... before finding the light.

2 I'm sorry you got so upset. We only hid your keys ....

3 It was no accident. She let the dog out ....

4 We'll either ring you with the results or let you know ....

5 We don't accept cheques without a card. You'll have to pay .... I'm afraid.

6 I'll need to get a new passport before we go. This one is ....

7 We hadn't planned to meet, we just saw each other there ....

8 I saw Chris .... here and gave him a lift home.

COMMUNICATIVE PRACTICE

1 Couch associations

This task is based on the psychological technique of word association: 'I'll say a word and you say the first thing that comes into your head . . . '

Look back at the chart you completed in Exercise 4 and write down eight of the phrases in box A below.

Box A   *Box B*

Working with another student, read out the phrases one at a time so that your partner has time to write down *the first word that comes into his/her head* (one word only) in response to each phrase. He/she should write these words in box B of his/her book.

When you have done this, your partner has to read back to you the words he/she has written *in random order* and you have to guess the association. Where an association is not clear to you, ask your partner to explain.

Now change roles so that you fill in box B.

What can you tell about the workings of your partner's mind from this task?

2 Two-joke puzzle

Below are two jumbled jokes. Working with another student, put the parts of the jokes into the correct order and complete the gaps with the appropriate prepositions. Each joke has been started for you.

Joke 1: A policeman was once . . .
Joke 2: A student was once sitting . . .

  1 .... duty in town when he noticed a pedestrian holding a piece of string,

  2 'Why?' replied his neighbour, without looking up. 'Have you only got nine?'

  3 .... a joke he decided to reveal a rather shocking piece of information to the student

  4 As this was not the sort of thing people usually do .... public, he asked,

  5 .... a library with his books

  6 sitting .... the desk next to him.

  7 which he was pulling along .... him.

  8 'If you look .... the desk for a minute

  9 'Why on earth are you pulling that along .... the street?'

  10 you'll see we've got 21 toes between us.'

  11 'Well,' he replied, 'I thought I'd look stupid trying to push it.'

  12 but was not .... a mood to work.

EXAM FOCUS

1 Cloze

Fill each of the numbered blanks in the following passage. Use only *one* word in each space. In line with the focus of this unit, all the blanks here are prepositions.

The warmth of the sun (1) .... the Athenian streets hints that summer is right around the corner, and with summer comes the internationally renowned Athens Festival. Every summer since 1955 the experience of watching drama, dance or music (2) .... the foot of the Acropolis (3) .... the open sky has captivated both residents and tourists.

   The Athens-based part of the Festival is (4) .... the ancient theatre of Herodes Atticus. It opens (5) .... Sunday 13th June with the Greek National Opera performing Georges Bizet's *Carmen*. Performances continue (6) .... 20th June. Among performers scheduled to appear (7) .... June are Marilyn Horne and the English National Ballet.

Some events have been added to those listed (8) .... the programme, but
organisers expect that even tickets for these additional events will have been sold
(9) .... next Friday. If you're planning to go (10) .... the Festival it is
advisable to check up-to-date programme changes with the Festival office.

(adapted from *Athenscope – The Weekly Guide to What's On in Athens*)

EXAM TIP 14

Look both ways

In the telegramese question, as in the cloze and
dialogue building questions, you have to 'look
both ways'. If you decide you need to add a
preposition, look both at what comes *before* and
after the preposition before you choose one.

- If it is a preposition of movement or place then
  what comes before, e.g. the verb, will usually
  guide your choice.
- If it is a prepositional phrase the word that
  comes after should guide your choice.

2 Telegramese

**Make all the changes and additions necessary to produce, from the following sets of
words and phrases, sentences which together make a complete letter. Write each sentence
in the space provided.**

Lesvos,
Greece

22nd August 1994

Dear Wendy,

1 I write / let you know / I arrive / England / Tuesday 29th.

  ....

2 I hope / you still meet me / the airport / as arrange.

  ....

3 I stay / my own / the moment / island of Lesvos.

  ....

4 Peter and Kim go / plane / another island / not be back until / Friday.

  ....

5 I sit / the sun / too long yesterday / I decide / stay here / myself.

  ....

6 We plan / head back / mainland / the weekend / stopping / few smaller islands / the way.

   ....

7 Kim / have to be / Athens / Monday afternoon / pick up / luggage.

   ....

8 I look forward / see you / cloudy Britain.

   ....

Love,
Claire

Unit 13 Modals 2

LEAD-IN

1 Look at Picture 1 and discuss the following questions with another student.

1 What do you think the man is going into the shop to buy?
2 How long do you think it will take him?

Picture 1

Now look at Picture 2. Working with another student, discuss what has happened.

Picture 2

2 Now discuss your views on each of the following questions using the language in the box.

couldn't have	must have	may have	could have	might not have
		+ past participle		

1 What happened to the car?
2 Was the woman by the tree involved in the car's disappearance? If so, how?
3 How about the man at the bus stop?
4 And the woman with the pram?
5 Is it possible that the other person in the picture wasn't what he / she seemed?

REFERENCE

Form

must	can('t)	could(n't)	may (not)	mightn't	
should(n't)	ought(n't) to	needn't			+ have + past participle

NOTES:

1 These forms cover both past simple and present perfect meanings.

You can't have seen him earlier. (I don't believe you saw him earlier.)
You can't have seen him already. (I don't believe you've seen him already.)

2 These forms do *not* exist in English: **didn't might, didn't should, mustn't have** + past participle.

A *Speculation and deduction about the past*

In Unit 2 we looked at how the modals **can, may, might, must, could, should** and **ought to** are used to talk about possibility, probability and certainty in the present and future. Here we shall look at how these modals are used to talk about the same ideas in the past.

Look at the table and write down how you express each form in your own language.

Must have expresses the speaker's certainty that something has happened.	*If he's not here by now he **must have** got lost.*	....
Could / may / might have express the idea that there is a possibility that something has happened.	*'He's very late. He **could have missed** the train.'* *'Or it **might have been** delayed.'*	....
Can't / couldn't have express the speaker's certainty that something has not happened.	*My father **can't have taken** the car; his keys are still here.*	....
May not / might not have express the idea that it is possible that something did not happen.	*No one's home. They **might not have received** the letter and **may not have been expecting** us.*	....
Should / ought to have can express the idea that:		
i) you expect something has happened but don't know;	*They **should have found** the message by now. I expect they'll ring soon.*	....
ii) you expected something to happen but it didn't.	*I'm not waiting much longer. She **should have been** here hours ago.*	....

> NOTE: **Can have . . .** is only used in questions.
> *Can she have found out about our plan, do you think?*

1 Complete each of the sentences with one of the modal verbs from the box below. Use all the verbs at least once.

should	couldn't	might not	must	could	ought to	can't

1 The car .... have been there to meet us. They promised it would be.

2 She .... have thought we were out. That's why she left a message.

3 .... Jeff have helped you? Didn't you ask him?

4 The package .... have arrived by now but I expect it's stuck in Customs.

5 They .... have seen the message; they would have rung if they had.

6 The police suspect that the couple .... have been using their real names.

7 She .... have gone away for the weekend but I doubt it.

8 Sue .... have bought any food this weekend. The fridge is absolutely empty.

9 Where do you think they .... have hidden the money?

10 You look great. You .... have had a really good time.

B *Obligation and necessity in the past*

In Unit 2 we also looked at how the modals **must, have to, should, ought to** and **needn't** are used to talk about obligation and necessity in the present or future. Here we shall look at how we use modals to talk about obligation and necessity in the past.

Needn't have + the past participle means that someone did something unnecessarily.	*You **needn't have paid** for a hotel. There's plenty of room here.* *We **needn't have gone** in fancy dress. Most people just wore their normal clothes.*
Didn't need to + the infinitive means that something was unnecessary, but it does not tell us if someone did this thing or not.	*He **didn't need to take** the medicine.* (It wasn't necessary to take it, but we don't know if he actually did.)
Didn't have to + the infinitive is similar to **didn't need to**, but is used more when the obligation comes from other people.	*The guard told us we **didn't have to wait** outside – we could go straight in.*
Should have + the past participle expresses the speaker's criticism of what someone has done.	*You **shouldn't have spoken to him** like that. It was very rude of you.*

2 Match either sentence (a) or (b) to the explanation on the right. Only one combination makes sense.

1 a) Rick didn't have to go to the meeting.
  b) Rick needn't have gone to the meeting.   The meeting was a waste of time.

2 a) Maria didn't have to stay at home.
  b) Maria needn't have stayed at home.   So she went out with a friend.

3 a) Simon didn't need to spend his money.
  b) Simon needn't have spent his money.   He got everything free.

4 a) Tina didn't need to do the homework.
  b) Tina didn't have to do the homework.   Her teacher made her, though.

COMMUNICATIVE PRACTICE

1 A moment in sport

Discuss with another student some of the kinds of sports the following words are used with:

match   tournament   race   meeting

Now look at pictures 1–8. With another student, first decide which sport is involved in each picture and then try and explain what has happened in each picture. You need to work out which piece of sporting action the photographer has caught.

Example:

A: *She's obviously a skier.*
B: *Yes, and she must have just turned. Look at the snow.*
A: *Yes, or she could have just stopped.*
B: *No, there's too much snow.*

2 What could they have meant?

English is an international language, which means that often people need to translate signs or instructions into English for foreign residents or travellers. Unfortunately, translators do not always manage to express what they intend.

Look at the following 'English' signs and notices that have appeared abroad and working with another student, try and work out what they must have wanted to say.

1 Please leave your values at the front desk. (*In a Paris hotel elevator.*)
2 In case of fire, do your utmost to alarm the porter. (*In a Viennese hotel.*)
3 Stop: Drive sideways. (*A detour sign in Kyushi Japan.*)
4 We take your bags and send them in all directions. (*In a Copenhagen airline ticket office.*)
5 Special today: no ice-cream (*In a Swiss mountain inn.*)
6 Visitors are expected to complain at the office between the hours of 9 and 11 a.m. daily. (*In an Athens hotel.*)
7 Our wines leave you nothing to hope for. (*On the menu of a Swiss restaurant.*)
8 Here speeching American. (*In a Majorcan shop.*)

(from a list compiled *Addison-Wesley*)

EXAM FOCUS

1 Multiple-choice

Choose the word or phrase which best completes each sentence. Circle A, B, C or D.

1 .... the match have finished already? It's only 3.45.
   A Can   B Must   C Ought   D Couldn't

2 The bus .... have come or I would have seen it.
   A mustn't   B might not   C can't   D shouldn't

3 They .... to have phoned us by now, don't you think?
   A had   B ought   C needed   D needn't

4 People .... do military service after the law was changed.
   A mustn't   B needn't   C didn't have to   D shouldn't have

5 It's really not worth waiting. They .... have been here hours ago.
   A should   B can   C needn't   D ought

6 He .... not have been joking about the change in starting time. Let's ring and check, shall we?
   A can   B could   C must   D might

7 You .... have bothered to bring me flowers, but it was very kind.
   A needn't   B didn't have to   C ought to   D must

8 'Did he have to get up so early?' 'No, he .... '
   A didn't have   B needn't have   C hadn't   D shouldn't

9 Those are her glasses on the table so I suppose she .... have arrived.
   A should   B couldn't   C would   D must

10 That .... have been mud on your trousers. Mud would have washed out.
    A can't   B must   C needn't   D may

2 Transformation

First decide which 'cue' in the box will help you to rewrite the sentence below. Then rewrite each sentence using the 'cue' so that it means the same as the printed sentence.

She must	She should	She may not	She didn't need	She could
She ought to	She can't	She might	She needn't	She couldn't

 1 It's possible she lost our address, I suppose.
    ....

 2 I'm sure she didn't have any idea about the surprise.
    ....

 3 I expected her to get here hours ago. Where is she?
    ....

 4 Perhaps she didn't know the dialling code for this area.
    ....

 5 I'm certain she took the car keys with her this morning.
    ....

 6 There was no need for her to take her passport so she left it at the hotel.
    ....

 7 She went to all that trouble for nothing because her friends didn't come in the end.
    ....

 8 According to her teacher she has probably passed the exams, but we'll know next week for sure.
    ....

 9 Maybe she was asked to stay on at work and that's why she's late.
    ....

10 I know she wasn't at the house then because she was with me.
    ....

Unit 14 **The passive**

Language focus: uses of passive; the 'agent' in passive sentences; causative structure: **to have something done**

Exam focus: transformation and dialogue building questions

LEAD-IN

1 In a passive sentence the person / thing doing the action is often not mentioned. This person / thing is called *the agent*.

Example: *Your arm will have **to be** bandaged properly.*
Probable agent: A doctor or a nurse.

Read the newspaper extracts below and discuss with another student who or what the probable agent is in each case, or whether the agent is unknown.

Debt drove man to crime

A man who planned an armed robbery to solve debt problems *was jailed* at the Old Bailey for 30 months yesterday.

1

Sheep flock to art gallery

Five sheep form part of an art exhibition opening next Thursday. The sheep which *have been* temporarily *coloured* will be at a gallery in Bond Street. The work is by Menashe Kadishman, an Israeli sculptor and former shepherd.

2

(from the *Independent*)

4,000 Ford jobs to go

FORD announced the loss of 4,000 jobs yesterday at the same time as the first Toyota *to be built* in Britain came off the production line.

3

Most senior citizen

DAISY ADAMS, of Church Gresley, Derbyshire, who *is believed* to be Britain's oldest person, celebrated her 113th birthday yesterday.

4

Accidental blaze

A fire which swept through a hostel in the North German town of Emstek *was* probably *started* accidentally, police said yesterday.

5

(from the *Guardian*)

2 Look back at the extracts in Task 1 and say why you think the agent was not mentioned in each case. Choose from these reasons:

A The agent is probably not known.
B The agent is obvious from the context.
C The agent is too vague to mention.
D The agent has already been or is likely to be mentioned later.

Match the explanations with the extracts.

REFERENCE

A *The passive*

Form

1 Active sentence: *Someone **broke into** our house last night.*
       subject   verb   object

   Passive sentence: *Our house **was broken into** last night.*
       subject   verb   agent (by someone) (not mentioned here because
                                                            not known)

2 The passive is formed with: the verb **to be** + past participle
   The passive is used in all tenses apart from the present perfect continuous and the future
   continuous.

1 **Complete each sentence with an appropriate form of the verb *to be* and then match each
verb to one of the tenses a–h below.**

1 I can't leave the house at the moment because our new carpet .... fitted.

2 The rubbish .... collected every Thursday morning.

3 The Treaty of Versailles .... signed in 1918.

4 As I entered the room, I had the feeling that I .... watched.

5 We had no idea that our luggage .... put on another plane already.

6 No decision .... taken about the vacant post yet.

7 If no one comes, all these preparations .... made for nothing.

8 The package .... sent to you by courier first thing tomorrow, I promise.

a) present perfect	d) past continuous	g) present continuous
b) past simple	e) present simple	h) future perfect
c) future simple	f) past perfect	

3 Other passive forms
   The passive can be used with modal verbs:

   *The forms **must be handed in** by Monday at the latest.*
   *The document **can't have been checked** for mistakes.*
   *We **might be fined** if we park here.*

   The passive can be used with **going to** and other verbs that take the infinitive with **to**:

   *Isn't the house **going to be repainted** next week?*
   *Michael **doesn't like to be disturbed** when he's studying.*

   The passive can also be used in the **-ing** form after main verbs:
   *I **can't stand being talked about** behind my back.*

Uses

1 The passive is used:

  a when it is not necessary to mention the doer of the action (the agent), e.g. in scientific experiments, or when the agent is not known.
  *The experiment **has to be done** in controlled conditions.*
  *Your seats **must have been double-booked**.*

  b very often in texts because of a change of focus between sentences.
  *A man in the crowd took out a gun and started firing. Four shots **were fired** altogether.*
  The subject of the second sentence is connected to the object of the first sentence.

  c in impersonal signs and notices and when talking about rules which apply to everybody:
  *Passengers **are not allowed** on the upper deck.*
  *Smoking **is forbidden** whilst moving around the plane.*

2 Match each piece of information below to the place in a–h where you are most likely to find it.

1 Contents should be kept in a dry place at all times.
2 Only to be pulled in an emergency.
3 To be continued . . .
4 Pieces must be moved in a clockwise direction.
5 Electricity can be generated in a number of ways.
6 Rooms must be vacated by 12.00.
7 Reserved.
8 You risk being cut off without further notice.

a) a plane
b) a television screen
c) a table
d) a door
e) a textbook
f) a packet
g) a bill
h) instructions for a board game

2 Special uses of the passive in impersonal phrases

We often use the passive when talking about what people generally say, **think, believe** or **know**.

Two different types of passive structure are possible:

Active: *People say that the Prime Minister is about to resign.*
Passive: ***It is said that** the Prime Minister is about to resign.*
Passive: *The Prime Minister **is said to be** about to resign.*

A similar use of the passive can be seen in the phrase *it is not known whether*.

***It is not known whether** the explosion was caused by a bomb.*

Where the action has already taken place, we use a perfect infinitive.

*The Prime Minister is believed **to have resigned**.*

B *Causative structure:* to have something done

There are certain actions that we do not typically or always perform ourselves. Instead, these actions are usually performed for us by professionals or specialists. To talk about such actions we can use the following structure:
'have + object + past participle'.

*We're going to **have the car serviced** before we go on holiday.*
*He's **had his hair cut** so short that I hardly recognised him.*

3 Write down two things that people typically have done in the following places.

Example: *At the dry-cleaner's you can have your clothes cleaned.*

1 the dentist's	3 the optician's	5 the hairdresser's
2 the shoe repairer's	4 a garage	6 the beautician's

COMMUNICATIVE PRACTICE

1 Fact triangles

The box below contains information about the people, places and things on the left.

Working with another student, find three relevant pieces of information for each subject. Connect the three pieces of information by drawing a triangle and then make sentences using the information, and the passive.

Example: *The Acropolis is made of marble.*
was built in 500 B.C.
was used as a temple.

1 John F. Kennedy

2 Napoleon

3 Australia

4 The Olympic Games

5 The First World War

6 Motion pictures

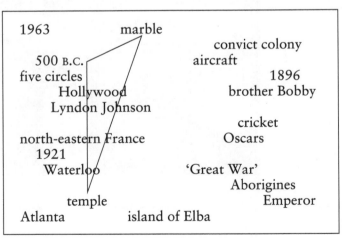

2 We've had everything done

Look at the two pictures of the house below *before* and *after* the Robinson family had everything done. Working with another student, discuss all the things the Robinsons have had done.

Example: *They've had new wallpaper put up.*

Then list the different people the Robinsons have paid to do the work. Write the different occupations in the box below.

Picture 1: Before

Picture 2: After

EXAM FOCUS

EXAM TIP 16

Redundant agents

In transforming passive sentences avoid including agents where they add nothing to the meaning of the sentence, e.g. words such as: **someone / anyone / people / something**, etc. Only include agents where the doer of the action is clearly identified, e.g. **by Mr Jones, by a total stranger.**

1 Transformation

Finish each of the following sentences in such a way that it means the same as the sentence printed before it.

1 People say that inflation is getting out of control.

 Inflation ....

2 Our water heater was repaired last week by the plumber you recommended.

 We ....

3 We'll have finished all the decorating by the weekend.

 All the decorating ....

4 The car ought to be looked at by a mechanic.

 You should ....

5 I hate it when people criticise me at work.

 I hate being ....

6 Someone should have informed her about the delay.

 She ....

7 The Customs official made us empty out our suitcases.

 We were ....

8 The council is building a new underground car park here.

 A new ....

9 The descendants of the Mina tribe still inhabit the island.

 The island ....

10 No one knows whether there are any survivors.

 It ....

EXAM TIP 17

An answer which fits the question

In completing the dialogue building question you
need to think carefully about how to *form* your
questions and answers. The context of the
dialogue may, for example, mean that you have
to form a question in the passive rather than the
active voice.

2 Dialogue building

**A guide is showing a group of students around Tremorovan Castle. Complete the
numbered gaps in the following conversation.**

Guide:	Now this room is the Great West Dining Hall which dates from a different period to the rest of the castle.
Student A:	When (1) .... ?
Guide:	The first stone wasn't laid here until 1632, almost eighty years after work started on the main site.
Student B:	(2) .... for?
Guide:	As the name suggests, the Duke intended to use it for great dinners and banquets but all kinds of events such as plays and concerts were held here. That's a portrait of the Duke of Tremorovan over there…
Student C:	When (3) .... ?
Guide:	In 1612, and he died in 1647, at the age of 35.
Student D:	How (4) .... ?
Guide:	Some say a witch put a spell on him but it was most probably scarlet fever.
Student E:	(5) .... as the Great Duke?
Guide:	Well, the people that lived in Tremorovan called him 'the Great Duke' because he was probably the first Duke in England not to demand rent from those who worked for him.
Student F:	(6) .... for the castle?
Guide:	He raised taxes while it was being built, mainly from tradesmen who would profit from the castle market.
Student G:	Why is the east wing closed?
Guide:	It (7) ....
Student G:	Restored?
Guide:	Yes. We had a fire here six months ago.
Student G:	How badly (8) .... ?
Guide:	There wasn't too much structural damage, but a few original paintings were lost.

Unit 15 **Word formation**

Language focus: meanings of prefixes and suffixes with adjectives, verbs and nouns
Exam focus: word formation and lexical gap-filling questions

LEAD-IN

A lot of words in English can be said to be related to each other because they contain the same root word, e.g. *clean – reclean – cleaner.* We usually think of a word like *clean* as the root word and the other words as being formed by adding prefixes or suffixes to it.

Prefixes indicate changes in meaning but do not usually indicate a change in the part of speech of the word, e.g. *clean* (v) – *reclean* (v); clean (adj) – *unclean* (adj).

Suffixes usually indicate a different part of speech, e.g.: *clean* (adj or v) – *cleaner* (n) – *cleanliness* (n).

1 Look at the headlines 1–6 and the extracts a–f below. Match each headline to an extract.

1 Washington party over-priced and over-crowded

2 Misdialled phone call 'led to attack by doctor'

3 BEATLES FOR CENTRAL PARK REUNION

4 Young giants of Japan outgrow weakling image

5 Police detain 107 illegal immigrants

6 'Healing Priest' last hope for incurably ill

b   The source was quoted as saying the concert was being backed by "an extremely wealthy, eccentric American".

a   Miss B said that she found herself speaking to Dr Courtney by chance

(from the *Independent*)

d   There have already complaints that the organisers have oversold, with many people grumbling that they have received nothing for the money that they have handed out.

c   He said three other men were found hiding on the roof of the lift.

(from the *Star*)

e   The legs of today's 17- to 18-year-old boys are 3.8 centlmetres longer than those of thelr fathers at the same age,

(from the *Guardian*)

f   Tales of cures for cancer, arthritis and other illnesses have earned Father Corsie Legaspi a church dispensation to set up a unique "healing ministry" to accommodate a growing number of believers.

2 The table below gives several prefixes. Find examples of words using these prefixes in the headlines above and write them in the *Examples* column. Next to each word write the part of speech it is: (n), (v), (adj) or (adv). Then complete the *Meaning* column with one of these meanings:

not   too much   bad(ly) or wrong   better / more than   again

Prefixes	Examples	Meaning
il-		
mis-		
over-		
in-		
re-		
out-		

REFERENCE

A *Adjectives*

1 The following prefixes all give the meaning of **not** when added to an adjective.

> dis-   il-   im-   in-   ir-   un-

Example: *That was **unfair** of you.* (**not** fair of you)

1 Match one of the prefixes in point 1 above to the words below.

1 loyal	4 honest	7 common	10 experienced
2 reliable	5 regular	8 polite	11 patient
3 legal	6 sincere	9 responsible	12 logical

2 The following suffixes can be added to a root word to form adjectives.

> -al   -ful   -less   -ous   -y

Example: *You mustn't be so **careless** with money.*

2 Use one of the suffixes in point 2 to make the adjective forms of the words below.

1 music	4 courage	7 success	10 advantage
2 risk	5 thought	8 danger	11 rust
3 help	6 stress	9 sleep	12 accident

NOTE: Some adjectives, such as **careful**, form the opposite with **-less**, e.g. **careless**. Some, such as **successful**, form the opposite with **un-**, e.g. **unsuccessful**.

Which of the adjectives you have just formed can be contrasted like this?

3 Other common adjectival endings are: **-ive**, **-ent**, **-able** and **-ic**. These endings are not simply added to the root words; the root itself is changed slightly when one of these endings is added.

Examples: *I am not particularly **confident** about the result.* (root word: **confidence**)
*He's quite an **aggressive** character.* (root word: **aggression**)

4 Many verbs have past and present participle forms which can be used as adjectives. For example **to tire: tired / tiring**. The **-ing** adjective form is used to talk about the general quality of the thing we are discussing.

*He's a really **boring** speaker. I hope I don't fall asleep.*

The **-ed** adjective form describes a person's reaction or response to the thing being discussed.

*She quickly became **bored** with the lecture and left.*

3 Complete each sentence with the correct form of the word given in brackets.

1 I found his new book really ....   (interest)

2 Most people left the concert feeling ....   (dissatisfy)

3 Hasn't he become .... since he started that job? He talks about nothing else.   (bore)

4 The children felt so .... about opening the presents that it took ages to get them to sleep.   (excite)

5 I thought she had some very .... arguments.   (convince)

6 Your new friend kept us .... all afternoon.   (amuse)

7 The person I sit next to just doesn't stop chatting which is .... if you're trying to work.   (annoy)

8 That's a film I don't particularly want to see. I've heard it's really ....
(depress)

B Verbs

1 Common verb prefixes are:

dis-	mis-	out-	over-	re-	under-

4 Discuss with another student the kinds of meaning these prefixes have when used with verbs. Then complete each sentence using one of the prefixes above, together with the verb at the end of the sentence.

Example: *Hotels on the island will soon be reopening after the winter break.*　　　OPEN

1 I'm sorry I'm late but the car .... in the traffic.　　　HEAT

2 The captain is in trouble again for .... an order.　　　OBEY

3 The prisoner is claiming that he was .... whilst in police custody.　　　TREAT

4 I'll never be able to eat all this. I think we've ....　　　ORDER

5 In the new plan, the library will be .... to another building.　　LOCATE

6 My team was completely .... by the opposition.　　　PLAY

7 I .... him because he has lied to us before.　　　TRUST

8 The repairs cost almost double what I thought they would. I really

.... how much damage was done.　　　ESTIMATE

2 Two common verb endings are **-en** and **-ise**.

-en is added to several adjectives and some nouns to give the verb form. Verbs formed in this way have the meaning of 'to make more . . .', e.g. **weaken**: 'to make weaker'. Other examples are:

harden	soften	sharpen	tighten	loosen	shorten	sweeten
frighten	lengthen	strengthen				

-ise is also a common verb ending. This ending is not simply added to the noun form; the noun itself is changed slightly when this ending is added, e.g.

sympathise	fantasise	dramatise	civilise	prioritise

C Nouns

1 Common endings for general or abstract nouns are:

-ity	-ness	-ment	-sion	-tion	-ism	-ing

After a few weeks at the school my feeling of **loneliness** *began to disappear.*

2 Common endings for personal nouns (nouns indicating people) are: **-er**, **-or** and **-ist**.
Napoleon adopted the title of Emperor of France.

5 Complete the following table with the correct nouns and verbs.

General noun	Personal noun	Verb
....	....	entertain
interpretation	....	....
....	....	manage
....	....	employ
....	typist	....
....	....	demonstrate
invention	....	....
....	....	compete

COMMUNICATIVE PRACTICE

1 Interpreting luggage

We can often tell something about people by the kinds of things they take with them on holiday. With another student, discuss the items and the titles of books that the four people below are taking with them and decide what sort of person you think each one is.

Thinking about the meaning of the highlighted prefixes and suffixes should help you identify each person.

PERSON A
- **re**chargeable batteries
- **un**leaded petrol vouchers
- **re**cycled writing paper
- *The Dis**appearing** Earth*

PERSON B
- sugar**less** biscuits
- coffee sweet**ener**
- **non**-fattening cheese
- *Over**eating***

PERSON C
- **un**marked essays
- **in**visible correction fluid
- **over**due library books
- *Children's **Mis**behaviour*

PERSON D
- **un**finished reports
- **in**complete accounts
- **un**answered letters
- *How to **Un**wind*

2 Situating signs

Look at the signs below and, working with another student, work out exactly where you might find them. Think carefully about the meaning of the prefixes.

EXAM FOCUS

EXAM TIP 18

Two types of knowledge

Word formation questions require you to spot:

- The *part of speech* that is needed in the blank – a noun, verb, adjective or adverb – and to think about the spelling of this word in connection to the word you are given.

- Whether you need to change this word *grammatically* to make it fit the sentence (make it plural, add a past tense ending, and a negative prefix, etc.).

1 Word formation

The word in capitals at the end of each of the following sentences can be used to form a word that fits suitably in the blank space. Fill each blank in this way.

1 My doctor gave me some very good .... for solving my back trouble.
ADVISE

2 Last year there were more than 15,000 .... who took part in the London Marathon.
COMPETE

3 I know Sarah wouldn't do anything .... ; she's much too nice a person.
HONEST

4 This knife won't cut anything, I'll have to .... it.
SHARP

5 I won't use that airline again, the air hostesses were most .... when we last travelled with the children. HELP

6 Learning to drive is one of the most .... things I've ever done. SATISFY

7 You owe Helen an .... for the things you said last night. APOLOGISE

8 When I went for the interview I .... got out on the third floor and spent ages outside the wrong door. ACCIDENT

9 Simon rides his bike to work now to .... on petrol. ECONOMY

10 I don't like the group's latest album, the music is just too .... REPEAT

2 Lexical gap-filling

Complete each sentence with a word that has the *opposite* meaning of the word in bold print in the sentence.

Example: *He was always a **loyal** colleague but proved to be a **disloyal** friend.*

1 Gambling is now **legal** in every part of the country, but there was a time when it was .... in most states.

2 I can never find a pair of trousers to fit. I always have to **lengthen** or .... them.

3 For brothers they're really unalike. Pete's extremely .... with his money whereas his brother couldn't be more **careful**.

4 We need someone **responsible** for this job but the records of these two candidates show that they're both too ....

5 The actor **appears** suddenly on stage and then .... in a cloud of smoke.

3 Lexical gap-filling

Complete each sentence with the word for the *name of the person* connected to the word in capital letters which follows the sentence.

Example: *All competitors must register at least one hour before the start.* COMPETE

1 You don't have to do that yourself. We employ a .... for that kind of work. TYPE

2 The police only arrested one .... in connection with yesterday's mass protests. DEMONSTRATE

3 My French isn't good enough for that kind of job. We'll have to get a professional .... in. INTERPRET

4 The electric light bulb was the last of this gifted .... 's long list of technological achievements. INVENT

5 We've taken on twenty new .... this year already. EMPLOY

125

Unit 16 Conditional sentences

> *Language focus:* uses of zero, first, second and third conditional forms; **if** and other conditional link words
>
> *Exam focus:* transformation question

LEAD-IN

1 Below are eight famous quotations which use conditionals. Working with another student, complete each quotation by matching the first half of the sentence on the left to the second half on the right.

1 If those of you in the cheap seats clap your hands, *f*

2 If you have nothing to say, *c*

3 If only I had known, *d*

4 If you give me six lines written by the most honest man, *e*

5 Lady Astor: 'If I were married to you, I'd put poison in your coffee.' *a*
Winston Churchill: 'If you were my wife,

6 How wonderful opera would be *g*

7 Playing Shakespeare is very tiring. You never get to sit down *b*

a) I'd drink it.

b) unless you're a king.
(*Josephine Hall, 1886–1957*)

c) say nothing!
(*Charles Caleb Colton, 1780–1832*)

d) I would have become a watchmaker.
(*Oppenheimer, the inventor of the atom bomb*)

e) I'll find something in them to hang him.
(*Cardinal de Richelieu, 1585–1642*)

f) the rest of you can just rattle your jewellery.
(*John Lennon, 1940–1980*)

g) if there were no singers.
(*Gioacchino Rossini, 1792–1868*)

2 The quotations above illustrate four types of conditional sentence. Look back at the quotations and complete the table below.

Quotation	If clause	Other clause
1, ...	....	.... or present simple
....	....	**will** + infinitive without **to**
....	past simple tense	....
....	....	**would have** + past participle

REFERENCE

1 Look at the phrases in the box below which describe the main uses of the zero and first conditional forms. Then read Sections A and B and complete sentences 1–3 in each section with the correct phrases from the box.

> giving instructions
> making offers / requests and promises / threats
> talking about things that are always true
> talking about people's typical reactions to situations
> talking about how future situations may develop

A *'Zero' or general conditional*

Form

If + present simple tense, present simple tense imperative

The words **when** and **whenever** can often be substituted for **if** with almost no change in meaning.

Uses

1 This form is often used when: *talking about things that are always true.*

White sugar **turns** a horrible black colour if it **is heated**.
Divers **get** dizzy when they **come** up to the surface too quickly.

2 This form is also used when:
Talking about peoples typical reactions to situations

He **gets** upset if I **mention** her name.
If I **don't have** breakfast, I **feel** terrible for the rest of the morning.

3 The imperative form is used in this structure when:
Giving instructions

Don't panic if you see a shark while diving.
If you get lost, **use** your whistle to call for help.

B *First conditional*

Form

If + present simple / present continuous tense, **will** + infinitive without **to**.

Can / may / could are used instead of **will** to express less certainty:

We **might** have to start without you if you're late.

Uses

1 We use this form when:
...... *talking about how future situations may develop* ......

If *we don't stay* in London, *I'll* probably have to change jobs.
There'll be trouble if Sheila *is coming* with Karen's ex-husband.

2 This form is also used when:
...... *making offers / requests + promises / threats* ......

We *won't* go back to work unless the pay offer *is improved*. — *Threat.*
Will you *help* out if we *need* another pair of hands? — *request*
I'll bring some extra chairs round if you *like*. — *offer*

C *Other words and phrases that can link conditional clauses*

Linking word/phrase	Meaning	Example
as long as / provided (that)	. . . but only if	I'll cook, provided that you wash up.
in case	to be prepared for the possibility that . . .	Bring your credit card in case the cashpoint isn't working.
otherwise	or (else)	Please hurry, otherwise we'll miss the start.
suppose	what if . . .	Suppose she's out – how will we get in?
unless	if . . . not	I'll call the police unless you pay.
whether		He doesn't know whether to go. It's a question of whether we can afford it.

2 Complete the sentences with a word or phrase from the table in Section C.

1 Don't sit like that .... you'll end up with back problems.

2 I won't go .... the company agrees to pay all expenses.

3 Simon ought to see a doctor .... he'll get worse.

4 .... you run out of money, what then?

5 Take my phone number just .... you need to ring me later.

6 I really can't decide .... it's worth going or not.

7 I'll go with you .... I don't have to do the driving.

8 Wait here a minute .... I'll introduce you to Karen.

D Other present tenses

> Use of the present continuous tense, the present perfect tense and the present perfect continuous tense is possible in zero and first conditional sentences.
>
> *Go and see a doctor, if you've been getting those headaches.* zero
> *I'll give you a key in case the bell isn't working again.* 1st
> *If she has had to work late again, I'll be really angry.* – zero

3 Look at the phrases in the box below which describe the main uses of the second and third conditional forms. Then read Sections E and F and complete sentences 1–2 in each with the correct phrases from the box.

> talking about imaginary results of past events
> talking about unreal / imaginary situations
> expressing regrets
> talking about less probable or unlikely future situations

E Second conditional

Form

If + past simple / past continuous tense, **would** + infinitive without **to**

Might and **could** can be used instead of **would** when there is more doubt in the speaker's mind.

Uses

1 We use this form when:

Talking about less probable or unlikely future situations

> *It would be great if you could come but I know time off is a problem.*
> *Suppose she won the election, do you think she'd keep her promises?*

2 The main use of this form is when:

talking about unreal or imaginary situations

> *If there were more space here, I'd ask you to stay with us.*
> *I wouldn't want to live anywhere else even if I had all the money in the world.*

NOTE: In such conditional sentences **were** is usually the preferred form of the verb **to be**, though **was** can also be used.

F *Third conditional*

Form

If + past perfect simple / continuous, **would have** + past participle

Uses

1 When we use the third conditional, we are always referring to something that either happened or didn't happen in the past but:

..............imaginary' results of past events..............

*If you **hadn't told** that man you spoke French, he **would** probably **have left** us alone.*
(But you did tell him.)

2 This form can have the meaning of:

..............expressing regrets..............

and is commonly used with the phrase **if only** in this sense:

*If only I'd **known** about your offer then, I **wouldn't have taken** this job.*

4 **Complete the sentences by putting an appropriate verb form in each blank. (One, two, three or four words.)**

1 If I ...had known... you were coming, I ...would have been... there to meet you at the station.

2 It's unlikely that she ...would have come... with us even if we paid for her ticket.

3 If you .... just a few close friends to the party, the place

.... left in the mess it's now in.

4 We ...would have been... here much earlier if we ...hadn't have got... lost on the way.

5 I .... on a long holiday if I .... you. You look as though you could do with a break.

6 If I ...had been the... prime minister at that time, I ...would have made... the same decision.

7 I'm not very optimistic about getting a loan. If you .... a bank

manager .... you lend us the money?

8 If only the trains .... running on time. We .... missed the first half of the match.

COMMUNICATIVE PRACTICE

1 Body language

Look at the gestures below and discuss with another student what you think they mean.

Example: *If someone makes the gesture in Picture 1, it probably means they . . .*
If someone does this, I think it means . . .

2 How would you get out of . . . ?

Imagine that you are in the three situations described below. Working with at least one other student, decide what you would say or do to get out of trouble.

Situation A

While babysitting for a friend you find a letter to her inside a magazine. It is from another friend and is very personal. You read it but accidentally spill coffee on it.

Situation B

You work in a shop. One Saturday night after closing time you realise you have left your purse or wallet inside and go back to get it, using your keys. When you leave you do not realise you've left your key in the door. That weekend several valuable items are stolen and the police are not sure how the burglars got in. If your boss finds out it was your key, she'll sack you.

Situation C

Your family is preparing a large surprise party for your grandfather's seventieth birthday. You have been given the job of doing the shopping but accidentally leave the enormous shopping list you have prepared somewhere where he sees it. He's very curious about the contents of the list.

Write your group's solution to each situation in large letters on a piece of card.

Example: B: *I'd say my bag had been stolen.*

Your teacher will then put the cards for each situation on the board. Say why your solution would be a better way to get out of the situation than any of the others.

One member of the class should be chosen to act as judge for each situation.

EXAM FOCUS

1 Transformation

Before rewriting the sentences with a conditional form, circle the form of the conditional you think you need to use. The numbers relate to the zero (0), first, second and third conditional forms looked at in the Reference section.

1 You only look so awful because you worry so much.

 If 0 1 2 3

2 The only reason I went was because Stephen was there.

 If 0 1 2 3

3 Would you like me to move my car?

 I 0 1 2 3

4 The taxi went the wrong way so Kate missed her flight.

 If 0 1 2 3

5 You're always blaming me for things that go wrong.

 Whenever anything 0 1 2 3

6 You might be delayed so I won't cook until you get here.

 In case 0 1 2 3

7 You don't do any exercise and that's why you put on weight.

 If 0 1 2 3

8 I didn't know you were back from holiday so I didn't phone.

 If 0 1 2 3

In sentences 9–14 the difficulty is not in choosing which conditional form to use but how using a different *link word* changes the pattern of the sentence.

9 You'll be alright as long as you keep to the path.

 Keep ....

10 They're still not sure if they're going to come.

 They can't decide ....

11 I don't mind driving long distances if the roads are good.

 As long as ....

12 You'll burn in this heat unless you put sun cream on.

 If ....

13 You should book your seats soon otherwise they'll all be sold out.

 If ....

14 If the firemen don't get here soon, there won't be a house to save.

 Unless ....

132

Unit 17 Verb and sentence patterns

Language focus: verbs followed by the **-ing** form, infinitive with **to**, or **that** clause; reported speech and tense changes; verbs and phrases followed by the infinitive without **to**

Exam focus: transformation and cloze questions

LEAD-IN

Looking in a good dictionary is usually one of the best ways to find out the kind of sentence pattern that typically follows a particular verb. Often important information is contained in the example sentences given.

Working with another student, complete the table about sentence patterns after verbs by reading the dictionary entries below. Put a √ if the sentence pattern can be used and an X if it cannot. Some have been done for you as examples.

Each verb can be followed by at least two different types of sentence pattern.

Finally, use the information in the dictionary entries to find an explanation for the uses of the different patterns with each verb.

1

tell /tel/ v **told** /təʊld/ **1** [T (about, of, to] to make (something) known in words to (someone); express in words: *If you knew you were going to be late, why didn't you tell me?\He's good at telling jokes.\Do you always tell the truth?\Tell me all about your new job.\The boss will have to be told about this.\He told us of his wonderful adventures in foreign lands.* [+obj(i)+obj(d)] *I always tell the children a story/tell a story to the children before they go to bed* [+obj+(that)] *John told us he'd seen you in town.* ... **2** [T] to cause (someone) to know what they must do; order; direct: *That child has got to learn to do what/as he's told* [+obj+wh-] *Don't try to tell me how to behave!* [+obj+to-v] *I told you to get here early, so why are you late?*

(adapted from the *Longman Dictionary of Contemporary English*)

2

(from the *Longman Dictionary of Contemporary English*)

try¹ /traɪ/ v **1** [I;T +to-v; obj] to make an effort or attempt (to do something): *I don't think I can do it, but I'll try.\If you don't succeed the first time, try again.\Don't criticize him too much; he's trying his best/his hardest.\He tried to stand on his head, but he couldn't.\The two sides are still trying to reach an agreement.\Try to get there on time.\I tried hard not to laugh when I saw his new haircut.* **2** (T+v-ing] to attempt and do (something) as a possible way of gaining a desired result: *If the car won't start, try pushing it.*

3

make If you make someone do something, you force them to do it. EG *You've got to make him listen... They were made to sit and wait for two hours.*

V+O+ INF:IF
PASS V+*to* INF
= compel

(from the *Collins COBUILD English Language Dictionary*)

Verb	+ -ing	+ infinitive with to	+ that clause	+ infinitive without to
tell			√	X
make			X	
try				

REFERENCE

A Verb + ing

1 These are some common verbs that are followed by the **-ing** form of another verb.

admit	**appreciate**	avoid	can't help	**can't stand**	consider	delay
deny	enjoy	**fancy**	feel like	finish	**hate**	**imagine**	**involve**
keep	love	mention	**mind**	postpone	practise	resist	**risk**
propose	suggest					

*You should **avoid taking** the A312 – it's always busy.*
*Haven't you **finished building** the wall yet?*

2 The verbs in bold print in the box above can also be used with the pattern:
'verb + object + **-ing** form'.

*You don't **mind us coming** along, do you?*
*I'll go as long as it doesn't **involve me hanging** around.*
*I can't **imagine not having** a computer at work now.*

NOTE: **Keep** has a different meaning when used with an object.

*He **keeps annoying** us.* (doesn't stop)
*He **kept us waiting** outside.* (made us . . .)

B Verb + *infinitive with* to

1 These are some common verbs that are followed by the infinitive with **to**.

afford	agree	allow	appear	arrange	ask	choose
expect	fail	help	hope	learn	manage	offer	pretend
promise	refuse	threaten	want			

*How can she **afford to go** on holiday twice a year?*
*We **expect to land** at approximately 1.45 local time.*

2 The following verbs are used with the pattern 'verb + object + infinitive with **to**'.

advise	allow	ask	encourage	expect	force	get	help
intend	invite	leave	order	persuade	prefer	remind	
teach	tell	want	warn				

*The guard only **allowed us to enter** after searching our bags.*
*Can I **remind you** once again **to take** all your belongings with you?*

(For more on object patterns see Unit 9.)

1 Match the parts of the sentences on the left to those on the right to make complete sentences which use the verb patterns described above.

1 I really can't imagine   a) coming out tonight, I suppose?
2 My doctor has advised   b) to do more exercise.
3 Could you remind your brother   c) people smoking.
4 There doesn't appear   d) her leaving without me.
5 Some people just can't help   e) me not to go out at all.
6 You don't fancy   f) to be any sign of them.
7 Hasn't she arranged   g) breaking into the car.
8 People ought to be encouraged   h) to be met by someone?
9 The boys consistently denied   i) to bring the cheque?
10 He really can't stand   j) making fools of themselves.

C Verb + -ing *or infinitive with* to

Some verbs can be followed by either the **-ing** form or an infinitive with **to**, usually with some difference in meaning. Some of these are given below in Exercise 2.

2 Look at the examples and explanations. Complete the explanations with either 'infinitive' or '-*ing* form'.

1 **need**

*I **need to go** to the hairdresser.*
*My hair **needs cutting** again.*

a) The .... is used when someone is going to do something.

b) The .... is used when something is going to be done.

2 **forget** and **remember**

*Don't **forget to feed** the cat.*
*I'll never **forget meeting** her.*
*I don't **remember seeing** him.*
*I hope you **remembered to feed** the cat.*

a) The .... is used to talk about past memories.

b) The .... is used when there is the idea of obligation.

3 **stop**

*We only **stopped to have** lunch.*
*I wish you'd **stop annoying** me.*

a) The .... is used when we mean 'to stop what one is doing'.

b) The .... is used when we mean **stop** 'in order to . . .'.

4 **begin**, **start** and **continue**

*She's **starting to get** tired.*
*We **started winning** halfway through the game.*
*He soon **began to lose** patience.*
*Perhaps we should **continue playing** tomorrow?*

The infinitive and the -**ing** form can both be used with no difference in meaning, but

only the .... is used after verbs in continuous tenses.

5 **try**

*I **tried to get** in but couldn't.*
*Try **ringing** Anne, she'll know.*

a) The .... shows that there is / was / may be some difficulty.

b) The .... shows that something is / should be easy to do.

6 **mean**

*I **didn't mean to hurt** anyone.*
*If it **means travelling** overnight, I'd rather not take the cheaper flight.*

a) The .... is used with the meaning 'involve'.

b) The .... is used with the meaning 'intend'.

D *Verb* + that *clause*

1 Some verbs are typically followed by a **that** clause:

argue	check	**complain**	explain	**insist**
say	wish (meaning 'prefer it if')			

*I **wish that** you would stop bothering me.*
*The Prime Minister **argued that** neither side was right.*

The verbs in bold print in the box can also, however, be used with an alternative preposition + the -**ing** form.

*He **complained about** having to wait.*
*He **insisted on not reporting** it to the police. (See also Unit 6.)*

2 These verbs, when followed by an indirect object, are then followed by a **that** clause:

admit	agree (with someone)	mention	pretend
promise	recommend	suggest	

> He *agreed with me* **that** *it would be difficult.*
> I *promised* her **that** *I'd arrive on time.*
> He *suggested* to us **that** *we tried a hotel.*

3 Some verbs which can be followed by either an **-ing** form or an infinitive with **to** can, in more complex sentences, be followed by a **that** clause.

> She *proposed having the meeting at a later date.*
> She *proposed* **that** *the meeting was postponed until everyone could attend.*
> He *reminded us* **to** *get there early.*
> He *reminded us* **that** *we should get to the cinema early as the film was very popular.*

E Reported speech and tense changes

When we report what people have said we may have to use a different tense from the one used by the speaker.

If the reporting verb is in the past tense (e.g. *he told me that* or *he mentioned that*) then what the speaker originally said usually changes tense, as follows:

Words spoken	*Words reported (She said that . . .)*
'Tom needs a rest.'	Tom needed a rest.
'Things are going well.'	. . . things were going well.
'He's lost weight.'	. . . he had lost weight.
'It was a great game.'	. . . it had been a great game.
'Karen was crying again.'	. . . Karen had been crying again.
'Oliver had done everything.'	. . . Oliver had done everything.
'I'll come round later.'	. . . she would come round later.

3 First look at sentences 1–10 and find a suitable way of reporting each one from phrases a–j. Then complete these sentences, paying careful attention to sentence patterns.

a) Simon suggested . . .   f) Lesley reminded . . .
b) Daniel argued . . .   g) Jim promised me . . .
c) Mr Jones threatened . . .   h) Sheila agreed . . .
d) Our neighbours have invited . . .   i) Mrs Winter complained . . .
e) The previous owners warned . . .   j) My doctor advised . . .

1 'You really ought to give up smoking.'

....

2 'I'll definitely pick you up before eight.'

....

3 'Let's take the cat back to the vet.'

....

4 'The rain gets in if you don't shut the window tightly.'

....

5 'You're right, it's too late to phone.'

....

6 '... but the atmosphere won't change unless conditions are improved.'

....

7 'I'll call the police if the noise doesn't stop.'

....

8 'Don't forget that they're one hour ahead in Spain.'

....

9 'Drop in any time you like.'

....

10 'The oven didn't work from the day we moved in.'

....

F *Verbs and phrases + infinitive without* to

Some verbs and phrases in English are followed by an infinitive without **to**.

make / let
*The guard **made** us empty our cases in front of him.*
*Why won't she **let** you come with us?*

had better
*We'**d better** not leave before the others get here.*

would rather
*I'**d rather** stay here than spend an hour walking to the beach.*

NOTE: The verb **prefer** has two very different patterns:
Usually: *My sister **prefers cycling** to walking.*
But after **would**: *I'**d prefer to eat in** rather than spend all that money at a restaurant.*

COMMUNICATIVE PRACTICE

1 Message in a mime

Work with another student. Imagine you are speaking to the people in the boxes below.

Think of a short message that you can mime or give with a gesture to each of the people in your box. Student A: Mime your messages to your partner, who writes down what he/she thinks he has been told, advised, offered, etc. Then see if he / she understood your message correctly.

Example:

A: *You were telling me that the smoke was bothering you, weren't you?*
B: *No. I told you that there was a 'No smoking' sign in the room.*

STUDENT A	STUDENT B
1 someone who is driving 2 someone who looks fed up 3 someone who is watching television 4 someone who is angry with you	1 someone who is smoking 2 someone who has given you the wrong change 3 someone who looks lost 4 someone who is parking a car

Student B: Now mime your messages to the people in your box in the same way.

2 Complete the captions

Working with another student, look at the cartoons below and complete the caption
below each one to highlight the humour in the situation. When you have finished you will
have a chance to compare your answers to those of the original cartoonist.

1

2

3 'I still think you should ask . . .'

'Please remember . . .'

'Please stop . . .'

4 'I just have this ability to make . . .'

5 'You need . . .'

6 'I told you that I'd rather . . .'

EXAM FOCUS

1 Transformation

Finish each of the following sentences in such a way that it means the same as the sentence printed before it.

1 'Why don't we go out to eat for a change?'

   Penny suggested ....

2 I'd prefer to go abroad on holiday this year.

   I'd rather ....

3 Were you upset that you weren't invited?

   Did you mind .... ?

4 After trying all day, I finally succeeded in getting Mr Fisher on the phone.

   I finally managed ....

5 I don't think you should go out with your cold.

   You'd better ....

6 'I'll make the country a safer place,' promised the Prime Minister.

   The Prime Minister promised ....

7 'The trip is not going to be an easy one,' said our teacher.

   Our teacher warned ....

8 I need to replace my two front tyres.

   My two front tyres need ....

9 They kept us waiting outside for nearly two hours.

   They made ....

10 I don't think you should drink the water: it looks dirty.

   I wouldn't risk ....

EXAM TIP 19

The verb predicts a sentence pattern

When doing a cloze question, remember that it is not just the words immediately either side of the blank that you need to look at. Every sentence has a verb and you should think about the kind of pattern that follows the verb.

2 Cloze

The following passage is about the day Queen Elizabeth II opened the doors of Buckingham Palace to the public. Fill each of the numbered blanks with *one* word.

Early visitors started a series of alarm bells (1) .... in Buckingham Palace yesterday by getting too close to an elaborate network of lasers and video cameras. Security men had to (2) .... running up and down stairs to check (3) .... the priceless royal treasures were intact.

Up to 8,000 people were (4) .... to form a queue outside but when the doors opened only 800 had turned up. Visitors were only (5) .... to see 20 out of the 600 rooms, but for the curious this newspaper can reveal some of the secrets they missed on the eight-pounds-a-head guided tour.

THE MOP ROOM – the room you'd probably fail to (6) .... as it's entered through a hidden door to the right of the throne. This is where one keeps one's vacuum cleaner and one's other bits and pieces like spare plugs.

THE POOCH ROOM – the ultimate in pet luxury. The royal dogs enjoy (7) .... to sleep on feathered mattresses after filling themselves with tinned dog food and biscuits.

Not all yesterday's visitors, however, went away happy. American tourist, Gene Harding, said that he prefers (8) .... to the White House where you get in free. Some people (9) .... about security guards turning them away or (10) .... them have a body search.

(from the *Daily Mirror*)

141

Unit 18 Review unit

Exam focus: cloze, transformation, word formation, dialogue building and telegramese questions

1 Cloze

See Exam Tips in Units 3, 5, 10 and 19.

The following passage is adapted from a booklet entitled *European Language Examinations*. It is a description of Paper 3 in the First Certificate exam.

Fill each of the numbered blanks with *one* word.

Candidates (1)......................... expected to demonstrate their knowledge and control of the language system (2) .... completing a number of tasks, some of (3) .... are based on specially-written texts.

There are five questions. The first four (4) .... are of (5) .... following task-types: gap-filling, transformations, word formation and sentence expansion.

The (6) .... question is a directed writing task. Candidates must write a concise response (7) .... an information-gathering or problem-solving task. Visuals (8) .... as charts and diagrams (9) .... accompany the task. Candidates must write their answers (10) .... relevant material.

(adapted from UCLES/ALTE, *European Language Examinations*)

2 Transformation

See Exam Tips in Units 12, 15 and 16.

The sentences in this exercise together make up 'Ten Useful Do's and Don'ts' when doing Paper 3.

Finish each of the following sentences in such a way that it means the same as the sentence printed before it.

1 Read the whole cloze passage before attempting any answers.

   The whole ....

2 You shouldn't write more than one word or give alternative answers in the gaps.

   Candidates are advised ....

3 Make sure you understand the context of the 'telegramese' letter before tackling each sentence.

Do not tackle ....

4 Finding correct answers in the cloze question may require you to look carefully at previous sentences.

You may ....

5 In the word formation question you must think carefully about which part of speech is required.

You need ....

6 If you don't put the written information in the 'guided writing' question into your own words you'll lose marks.

Unless ....

7 Check your spelling of words in the word formation question after completing the question.

Once you ....

8 When filling in a line of dialogue, your answers must fit with both the line before it and the line after.

Each ....

9 You may have to add a prefix in changing words in the word formation question.

A prefix ....

10 Think about what part of speech was possible in the blanks in the cloze.

Think about what part of speech each word could ....

3 Word formation: Classic spelling mistakes!!!!

See Exam Tips in Units 4 and 18.

Spelling words correctly is important to your success in this exercise. The words have been chosen because they typically cause learners problems. Before filling each blank, think about what the spelling difficulty might be with the word you have been asked to find.

The word in capitals after each of the following sentences can be used to form a word that fits suitably in the blank space. Fill each blank in this way.

1 You are .... to take plenty of warm clothes with you.   ADVICE

2 The politician made an unexpected .... on the show.   APPEAR

3 Keep your .... because you can claim for expenses.   RECEIVE

4 Our country has been .... forgotten by the rest of the world.   TRAGIC

5 The .... of that piece of music is a genius.   CREATE

6 I didn't like the person .... to represent the staff. CHOICE

7 It's by far the .... country I've ever been to. HEAT

8 We'd go out of business if we gave money back to every .... customer. SATISFY

9 To transfer a call, ... dial the number and put the phone down. SIMPLE

10 His story is ridiculous and quite .... BELIEF

4 Dialogue building: Interview with an examiner

See Exam Tips in Units 1, 13 and 17.

Complete the numbered gaps in the following conversation. It is an extract from an interview with an examiner for the First Certificate examination, who is talking about the marking of Paper 3.

Interviewer: What's the most common question you are asked as an examiner?

Examiner: That's easy. Everybody wants to know about Paper 3 and how (1) ....
....

Interviewer: So what is the secret of the marking?

Examiner: There's no secret, it's just quite complicated. Take the cloze question for example. Students should not write more (2) ....

Interviewer: Yes, it says that in the instructions but what happens (3) .... ?

Examiner: It depends. If both alternative answers are possible, they still get the mark. If one is wrong, they lose the mark.

Interviewer: What about spelling? Do students lose a mark if they (4) ....
.... ?

Examiner: Again, it depends. In a question like the word formation one, where spelling is being tested, they do. In other questions they may not.

Interviewer: Is every single item worth one mark or are some (5) ....
.... ?

Examiner: In a question like the telegramese, one item – one sentence, that is – may be worth three or four marks, depending on how many changes or additions students (6) ....

Interviewer: And what about the guided writing question? What advice (7) .... students here?

Examiner: Two things. Firstly, students must answer the question appropriately, using but not copying the relevant information and secondly, the language they use must be accurate and reasonably varied.

Interviewer: Another thing I've always been interested in is the number of marks for each paper. Is Paper 3 worth the same number of marks as (8) ....

.... ?

Examiner: Not quite. Papers 1, 2, 3 and 5 count for approximately 22 per cent of the total score each, whereas Paper 4 counts for approximately 12 per cent.

5 Telegramese: Dear Candidate

Make all the changes and additions necessary to produce, from the following sets of words and phrases, sentences which together make a complete letter. Write each sentence in the space provided.

See Exam Tips in Units 2, 7, 9, 11 and 14.

Dear Candidate,

1 You be / about take / Paper 3 / First Certificate examination.

....

2 Exam last / two hours / you try / complete all questions.

....

3 You be advised / leave some time / check what / you write.

....

4 Candidates do best / in exam / be those / think / what a particular question / test.

....

5 Do not / write / first thing / come / your head.

....

6 In cloze / word formation question / first consider / part of speech / need the blank.

....

7 In transformation / dialogue building question / work out / the grammar point / behind question.

....

8 I hope / you find / this book / useful / help you / prepare exam.

....

9 I look forward / see you / pass.

....

Yours faithfully,

The Author

Irregular verbs

infinitive	past simple	past participle	infinitive	past simple	past participle
be	was / were	been	mean	meant	meant
beat	beat	beaten	meet	met	met
become	became	become	pay	paid	paid
begin	began	begun	put	put	put
bend	bent	bent	read /ri:d/	read /red/	read /red/
bet	bet	bet	ride	rode	ridden
bite	bit	bitten	ring	rang	rung
blow	blew	blown	rise	rose	risen
break	broke	broken	run	ran	run
bring	brought	brought	say	said	said
build	built	built	see	saw	seen
burst	burst	burst	seek	sought	sought
buy	bought	bought	sell	sold	sold
catch	caught	caught	send	sent	sent
choose	chose	chosen	set	set	set
come	came	come	sew	sewed	sewn / sewed
cost	cost	cost	shake	shook	shaken
cut	cut	cut	shine	shone	shone
deal	dealt	dealt	shoot	shot	shot
dig	dug	dug	show	showed	shown
do	did	done	shrink	shrank	shrunk
draw	drew	drawn	shut	shut	shut
drink	drank	drunk	sing	sang	sung
drive	drove	driven	sink	sank	sunk
eat	ate	eaten	sit	sat	sat
fall	fell	fallen	sleep	slept	slept
feed	fed	fed	speak	spoke	spoken
feel	felt	felt	spend	spent	spent
fight	fought	fought	split	split	split
find	found	found	spread	spread	spread
fly	flew	flown	spring	sprang	sprung
forbid	forbade	forbidden	stand	stood	stood
forget	forgot	forgotten	steal	stole	stolen
forgive	forgave	forgiven	stick	stuck	stuck
freeze	froze	frozen	sting	stung	stung
get	got	got	stink	stank	stunk
give	gave	given	strike	struck	struck
go	went	gone	swear	swore	sworn
grow	grew	grown	sweep	swept	swept
hang	hung	hung	swim	swam	swum
have	had	had	swing	swung	swung
hear	heard	heard	take	took	taken
hide	hid	hidden	teach	taught	taught
hit	hit	hit	tear	tore	torn
hold	held	held	tell	told	told
hurt	hurt	hurt	think	thought	thought
keep	kept	kept	throw	threw	thrown
know	knew	known	understand	understood	understood
lay	laid	laid	wake	woke	woken
lead	led	led	wear	wore	worn
leave	left	left	win	won	won
lend	lent	lent	write	wrote	written
let	let	let			
lie	lay	lain			
light	lit	lit			
lose	lost	lost			
make	made	made			